CHILD WELFARE OUTCOME RESEARCH IN THE UNITED STATES, THE UNITED KINGDOM, AND AUSTRALIA

BY ANTHONY N. MALUCCIO
FRANK AINSWORTH
JUNE THOBURN

CWLA PRESS • WASHINGTON, DC

CWLA Press is an imprint of the Child Welfare League of America. The Child Welfare League of America (CWLA), the nation's oldest and largest membership-based child welfare organization, is committed to engaging all Americans in promoting the well-being of children and protecting every child from harm.

CHILD WELFARE LEAGUE OF AMERICA, INC.
440 First Street, NW, Third Floor, Washington, DC 20001-2085
E-mail: books@cwla.org

CURRENT PRINTING (last digit)
10 9 8 7 6 5 4 3 2 1

Cover design by Tung Mullen
Text design by Peggy Porter Tierney

Printed in the United States of America
ISBN # 0–87868–918–4

Library of Congress Cataloging-in-Publication Data
Maluccio, Anthony N.
    Child welfare outcomes research in the United States, United
  Kingdom, and Australia/
  Anthony N. Maluccio, Frank Ainsworth, June Thoburn
      p. cm.
    Includes bibliographical references.
    ISBN 0-87868-918-4
      1. Child welfare--United States--Evaluation. 2. Child welfare--Great
  Britain--Evaluation. 3. Child welfare--Australia--Evaluation.
  4. Evaluation research (social action programs)--United States.
  5. Evaluation research (Social action programs)--Great Britain.
  6. Evaluation research (Social action programs)--Australia. I. Ainsworth,
  Frank. II. Thoburn, June. III. Title.

HV741 .M343 2000
362.7--dc21

                                                              00-045548

Contents

Preface v

1 Overview of Outcome
   Research in Child Welfare 1

2 Outcome Research on
   Traditional Services 15

3 Outcome Research on
   Recent Service Initiatives 69

Conclusion 107

Appendix: Texts on Child
Protective Services 111

References 117

About the Authors 145

Figures

Figure 1. Components of Outcome
           Research in the Human Services 2

Preface

This volume reviews the bodies of outcome research about child welfare programs from the United States, the United Kingdom, and Australia, particularly outcomes in relation to service effectiveness, duration of child placement, permanency planning, and child development and functioning. The intention is to give child welfare administrators, policymakers, practitioners, and academics in each of these countries a comprehensive picture of the current state of child welfare knowledge, at least in the English-speaking world.

The volume begins with a discussion of issues in carrying out outcome research and consideration of the different service systems in the three countries. It then covers outcome research in a range of areas, as depicted below:

Traditional Services:
Kinship care
Family foster care
Treatment foster care
Residential group care
Adoption

More Recent Service Initiatives:
Family preservation
Family reunification
Preparation for independent living
Looking After Children
Family group decisionmaking
Shared family care
Wraparound services

Child abuse and neglect/child protection services, which constitute a substantial component of child welfare services, are touched on but not explored in detail. Outcome research in this area is reviewed or summarized in a number of recent volumes, and an annotated list is included in the Appendix. It should also be noted that the child protection literature is often integral to the child welfare literature, particularly in Britain.

Anthony N. Maluccio
Frank Ainsworth
June Thoburn

Chapter 1

Overview of Outcome Research in Child Welfare

Outcome Research in the Human Services

In an ideal world, there would be a close interaction between research and practice in the human services. Above all, program planning and implementation would be carried out rationally as a result of such interaction, as well as the findings of outcome research (Fein & Staff, 1993). By "outcome" research we refer, in particular, to quantitative and/or qualitative studies that examine the efficiency and effectiveness of services and programs designed to enhance the functioning of client groups coming to the attention of human service agencies.

We are especially interested in studies that contribute to the knowledge base of social work and other human service professions. Fein and Staff (1993, p. 210) underscore a major reason for this:

> Although decisions on implementing, maintaining, or expanding programs may be based, in reality, on emotional and political instincts, those instincts are best informed when a solid information foundation exists. Data can originate from evaluation studies of effort, effectiveness, efficiency and adequacy.

There is an extensive body of outcome research in the human services in the countries under consideration: the United States, the United Kingdom, and Australia. Most studies reflect one or more of the following components, as outlined in Figure 1 (Turner, 1993, p. 182), "goals, inputs, operations, quantity of output, quality of output, and client and case outcomes."

Much of this research is summarized in such volumes as Bergin and Garfield (1994) and Boss et al. (1993) in the U.S.; Sellick and

Figure 1.
Components of Outcome Research in the Human Services

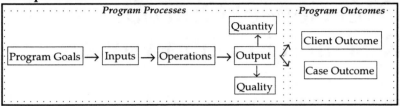

Source: *Evaluating Family Reunification Programs,* p. 182, by J. Turner (1993). In B.A. Pine, R. Warsh, & A.N. Maluccio (Eds.), *Together again: Family reunification in Foster Care* (pp. 179–198). Washington, DC: Child Welfare League of America. Reprinted with permission.

Thoburn (1996) and Stevenson (1999) in Britain; and Fernandez (1996), Goddard (1996), and Goddard and Carew (1993) in Australia. The reader is referred to the above texts for review of outcome studies in each of the above countries. Also useful is a special issue of *Smith College Studies in Social Work* entitled "Clinical Practice Evaluation: Conceptual Issues, Empirical Studies, and Practice Implications (Drisko, 2000), which includes articles pertaining to child welfare and family services.

Outcome Research in Child Welfare

An ongoing task for researchers is assessment of the effectiveness of services in such a vast, complex, and varied field as child welfare. This is a daunting task, especially in light of rapidly changing opportunities and challenges.[1] In particular, the challenge of conducting rigorous evaluation of innovation in the human services remains a worthy but elusive goal. A considerable amount of outcome research is going on in the U.S. and Britain and to a lesser extent in Australia; many of the studies, however, involve small data sets and therefore make limited use of statistical techniques to attempt to explain differences in outcome. In this volume we group together these smaller studies and provide a commentary of what they appear to be suggesting collectively about the impact of a range of variables on outcome. Only the most robust or substantive of the studies are described in more detail.[2]

In examining these findings, it is important to note the difficulties inherent in doing quantitative research and in following the scientific method as originally developed for the physical sciences. In this connection, we should point out that child welfare research is moving beyond the traditional exploration of discrete factors and toward emphasis on the interactive processes that affect children and their families. Such a shift promises to contribute to the quest of researchers, policymakers, practitioners, and educators for pertinent and effective principles and guidelines (Fein et al., 1990). There is, moreover, agreement that the field should be committed to a comprehensive research agenda, as outlined by contributors to a special issue of *Child Welfare* (Curtis, 1994), which addresses the following themes:[3]

- The field of child welfare needs knowledge that is derived from rigorous research.

- The field is being challenged to make good use of vast data that will be gathered as a result of marked progress in information systems and technologies.

- Increased attention to issues of accountability and outcome evaluation will substantially influence the delivery and administration of child welfare services in the future.

- Research must be culturally competent and account for the special needs of minorities.

In regard to the last theme above, outcome research—particularly in the U.S.—needs to pay more explicit attention to the dimensions of race and ethnicity (Courtney et al., 1996; Ewalt, Freeman & Fortune, 1999; and Iglehart & Becerra, 1995). In this connection, Pinderhughes (1997, p. 20) asserts that, "Training practitioners for competence with diverse populations is high on the list of corrective initiatives to address. . . inadequacies" in social work practice. Clearly, a similar point could be made about the training of researchers.

Although there is a growing mandate to conduct rigorous evaluation, researching outcomes of child welfare interventions is complex for many reasons. It is difficult to compare different studies, which use different outcome measures, different ways of describing process, and include data on very different sorts of children with differing needs in different types of placement. It is, therefore, not surprising that our attempt to compare outcome research in this volume is even more complex when we cross national boundaries. For instance, "family preservation services" in the U.S. would come under the general heading of "family support" or "preventive" services in the U.K. The British model of child welfare work makes the assumption (though it does not always happen that way) that a child and family social worker will work with family members to coordinate a range of services according to family needs, as is envisaged by the term "wraparound services" in the U.S. Interventions such as family foster care and treatment fostering merge, as do long-term or "permanent" foster placement services and adoption services. A small children's home offering long-term care to children with special needs may be more like a permanent foster home, and a task-centered foster home may have more in common with a group care setting than with a traditional long-term foster placement.

Issues of reliability and validity of data are especially crucial, as demonstrated by Folman's (1998) extensive study of the functioning of children in foster care. Along with intensive interviews, this investigator employed a variety of scales—particularly the Achenbach Child Behavior Check List (Achenbach, 1991)—that rely on children's self-reports as well as reports by parents, foster parents, and teachers. Folman found that, although these scales have been reported to be highly reliable in studies of both normative and high-risk populations, they have limited reliability and validity when administered to a foster care population. For example, foster children in her sample revealed numerous problems and vulnerabilities, even though according to the results of standardized tests they were functioning relatively well. It was evident that findings from "respectable" measures such as the Achenbach tool may have little correspondence with the realities of a child's life as revealed in in-depth interviews. Folman therefore concluded that, by focusing primarily on scale scores, we may miss the unique meaning of foster children's responses. Thoburn, Norford, and Rashid (2000) make a similar point about disruption rates as the main or only outcome indicator of the success of permanent family placement.

Even if there can be clarity about outcomes and processes, there are many variables outside the control of those providing services, which may have an impact on the outcomes for the child and family. These include characteristics of the children (including their early history); characteristics of the birth family and relatives and the environment (including schooling) before the child welfare services came into play; characteristics of foster carers or other resource providers, and, not least, the temperament of the child: is this a resilient child or a particularly vulnerable child? This range of variables makes it difficult enough to consider the impact of any particular intervention on outcome if the outcome is measured within a fairly short time scale. Thus, in family preservation services, if a particular mode of behavior is causing problems to the child and family, it might be possible to institute a behavioral program that might anticipate some change in the child's behavior within a fairly short time scale. It might therefore be possible to control for some intervening variables within this time scale. However, when a child is placed at six weeks for adoption, one cannot determine outcome until the child is in his or her mid-20s. Consider the number of intervening variables during this 25-year time span. Whether or not a particular method of preparing the adopters is associated with a positive outcome when so many other variables intervene one cannot possibly say.

Another issue is that, in Australia, child welfare policymakers, practitioners, and academics are frequently faced with journal articles and other publications that present the empirical results of British or American outcome research. Unfortunately, British authors frequently only cite the British research, and American authors cite only the American research. This is an unsatisfactory situation, since neither perspective presents the sum available knowledge about key child welfare issues.

Additionally, both Australia and the U.K. tend to import program initiatives from other countries without review of the available research evidence that supports or questions these initiatives and without full consideration of differences in context and culture. Recent examples are family preservation services (FPS) and wrap-around services (WS) from the U.S., the Looking after Children

(LAC) scheme from Britain, family group conferences (FGC) from New Zealand, and (for the U.K.) "concurrent placements," "solution focused therapy" from the U.S., and FGCs from New Zealand. Often there is also a significant time lag before research results about these new initiatives reach Australian policymakers and practitioners. The consequence is that new state or nongovernment services are often based on the first wave of enthusiasm for these initiatives rather than on the mature appreciation of the most recent research evidence about their effectiveness. In addition, when these new initiatives are embraced, differences in social values and the service systems among the U.S., U.K., and Australia are sometimes not fully recognized (Ainsworth, 1993; Scott, 1993).

Child Welfare Service Systems in the U.S., the U. K., and Australia

This section outlines the child welfare service system in the U.S., the U.K., and Australia. This is done in order to give the reader some understanding of the different cultural contexts in which these services are provided. This should also ensure that readers are aware of how the context may affect the research questions and findings.

From the U.S.

Although there are pertinent federal laws and regulations, for the most part child welfare services in the U.S. are governed by state laws and administered by state, county, or local jurisdictions. Services are delivered by state departments or their divisions, with names such as "Family and Children's Services," "Children and Youth Services," and "Children, Youth, and Families." These agencies work, in varying degrees, with other public agencies in such areas as health and mental health, income maintenance, and juvenile justice.

Federal laws and regulations influence the delivery of child welfare services, through a range of requirements for obtaining funding and reimbursement from the federal government. The primary federal laws, described in detail by Pecora, Whittaker, Maluccio and Barth (2000), include:

- The Child Abuse Prevention and Treatment Act of 1974 (P.L. 93-247), which provides financial assistance for prevention and treatment programs.

- The Indian Child Welfare Act of 1978 (P.L. 95-608), which recognizes tribal courts as having jurisdiction in child welfare issues involving American Indians and promotes placement of American Indian children with their kin or other tribal families.

- The Adoption Assistance and Child Welfare Act of 1980 (P.L. 96-272) and its successor, the Adoption and Safe Families Act of 1997 (P.L. 105-89), which regulate permanency planning for children who are neglected or abused—or at risk of neglect or abuse by their families.

- The Family Preservation and Support Services Act of 1993 (Public Law 103-66), and the Promoting Safe and Stable Families Program of 1995 (Public Law 105-89), which stress the safety of children, promote adoption and other permanent homes, and support birth families.

- The Multiethnic Placement Act of 1994 (P.L. 103-382) and the Interethnic Adoption Provisions Act of 1994 (P.L. 104-88), which forbid agencies receiving federal funds from making foster care and adoption placement decisions routinely on the basis of race, culture, and ethnicity.

Public agencies typically collaborate with private, not-for-profit organizations through contracting out on a fee-for-service basis. In recent years, this pattern has been increasing, especially in such areas as child mental health and juvenile delinquency. Moreover, since the 1960s, there has been a steady increase in the numbers of voluntary agencies—sectarian and nonsectarian—that depend largely or entirely on government contracts and subsidies for their survival. This is a dramatic change from earlier decades, when voluntary agencies were able to support most services through their endowments and/or charitable contributions.

In short, child welfare in the U.S. is characterized by complex problems at the service delivery and legislative levels. At present, it appears that "shifts in federal policy point toward curtailed child welfare spending and dispersed responsibility among states and counties for child welfare services" (Brooks & Webster, 1999, p. 297). In addition, a complex interaction between welfare reform and service delivery is emerging in child welfare—an interaction that is evolving and not clearly understood.

From the U.K.

As reflected below, there are substantial differences in public and private laws pertaining to child welfare in the various countries of the U.K. The laws are the same for England and Wales but different for Scotland and Northern Ireland. Also, statistical data are produced separately for every country; data included in this volume pertain primarily to England, for which numbers are substantially larger than for other parts of the U.K.

Child and family social work practice in England and Wales is principally regulated by the Children Act 1989, which is firmly rooted in the UN Convention on the Rights of the Child.[4] The Children (Northern Ireland) Order 1995 makes almost identical provisions, but the Children (Scotland) Act 1995 has important differences. With the arrival of devolved government in Scotland, Northern Ireland and, to a lesser extent, Wales, differences among the four parts of the United Kingdom are likely to increase. Recent developments in child welfare law, policy, and practice are described in Hill and Aldgate (1996).

The social care division of the Department of Health in England and the Scottish, Northern Irish, and Welsh Assemblies play a key part in setting policy and quality standards, the overall level of resources, and in monitoring their impl3mentation in practice. Following recent criticism of standards for children cared for away from home (Department of Health, 1997b), additional funding has been provided to meet a set of "Quality Protects" standards and performance indicators (Department of Health, 1998). The reports of the Social Services Inspectorate on different aspects of the work of individual Social Services Departments are rich sources of evaluative data. The provision of services is delegated to local authority Social Services

Departments in England and Wales, Social Work Departments in Scotland, and Health Care Trusts in Northern Ireland.

The Children Act 1989 (England and Wales) requires local authorities to provide a range of services for children "in need," defined at the broadest level as those under the age of 18 "who are unlikely to achieve, or to have the opportunity of achieving, a reasonable standard of health or development without the provision of services under this Act" (Section 17 (10) b). These services, now known as "family support" services, are to be provided to a child assessed as "in need" and may also be provided to any member of the family, as long as to do so will benefit the identified child. The local authority is given the responsibility of deciding the exact range and volume of services to meet local requirements, but guidance sets the broad parameters; suggests they will include social casework, advice, therapy, practical help such as domiciliary help and day care; and establishes that they will be delivered from a range of settings, including family centers. Services may be provided directly by local authorities or they may enter into agreements with private or voluntary agencies. A "mixed economy" of provision is encouraged. There is a strong emphasis on working in partnership with the other statutory agencies (education, health, police, housing) not only, as has long been the case, for the provision of child protection services, but for all their services. To that end, each local authority is required to provide an annually updated, multidisciplinary "Children's Services Plan," and there is provision for "joint funding" and "joint commissioning" of services across departmental boundaries.

Children placed in out-of-home care at the request of their parents are "accommodated." Importantly, short- or long-term "accommodation" is to be seen as an important aspect of family support rather than something to be prevented, as was previously the case. Only those children for whom the courts make a full or interim care order are "in care," and even with these, the parents retain some elements of "parental responsibility," which is only totally ended by an adoption order. The term "looked after" is used to describe both children who are "accommodated" and those on "care orders."

The threshold for making a care order is that a child is suffering or is likely to suffer "significant harm"; that the harm is attributable to deficits in parental care; and that making an order will be better for the child than not doing so. The emphasis throughout the Act is on working cooperatively with parents and only using coercion when the child's best interest requires it. Throughout the guidance there is an emphasis on seeking to work in partnership with parents, relatives, and children, and the Department of Health (Department of Health, 1995b) practice guide, *The Challenge of Partnership in Child Protection*, gives detailed advice on how this might be achieved. Parents and children who are old enough must be consulted before they are looked after and before important decisions are made, and "due consideration" has to be given to their wishes. For all "looked after" children, there is the presumption of continuing contact between parents and close relatives and the children and detailed guidance about how this is to be facilitated. Courts may make "contact orders" if arrangements cannot be sorted out without their intervention, and can also make orders for "no contact" if it can be demonstrated that this is necessary to secure the child's short- or long-term welfare or protection.

From Australia

Australia is a federation of states and territories, and child welfare services are a state or territory responsibility. There is no national child welfare legislation, and legislation on these matters varies among states and territories. For example, all states and territories except for Western Australia have mandatory reporting of child abuse and neglect; the designation of which occupational groups are bound by mandatory reporting, however, varies among the different states and territories (Zabar & Angus, 1994).

Child welfare services are also delivered by state departments that have various names. In Western Australia, there is the department of Family and Children's Services, while in New South Wales, the responsible department is Community Services. In some states, for example New South Wales, disability services and child welfare are combined in one department, the Department of Community Services. On the other hand, in Western Australia, there is a separate Disability Services Commission. A further complication is that, in some instances, mega departments exist, such as Victoria's Department of Health and Human Services, that cover the health sector, child welfare, and disability services.

Two unusual and, in some measure, contradictory developments that date from the 1980s are the Australian government's financial support for the development of child care services, and the national Supported Accommodation Assistance Program (SAAP). The latter program provides a substantial number of hostel-type services for homeless youth. The result of the child care initiative is that family-based or center-based child care services are subsidized by the national government through the federal department of Health and Human Services. For administrative purposes, the funds to support these services are channeled through state and territory governments. State and territory departments usually regulate and accredit these programs and their practitioner workforce. For example, in Western Australia there is a legally constituted Child Care Board that undertakes this task. Local city, town, or shire councils also have access to these monies, and as a result child care services of this type are in evidence at a local level. Private for-profit child care centers also exist. These agencies have access to fee subsidies from the national government for those needy parents who use these services. Services of this type are also provided on a similar basis by not-for-profit, nongovernment voluntary organizations.

The situation in regard to the SAAP programs is similar, although there is no comparable legally constituted board that regulates programs or accredits the practitioner workforce (Ainsworth, 1998). Services of this type are invariably auspiced by not-for-profit, nongovernment voluntary organizations and community-based youth groups. National funds for these services are channeled through state and territory governments in a similar manner to those for child care. A recent census of 1,183 SAAP services indicates that there are approximately 14,000 homeless young people aged 15–19 years served by these programs (Australian Institute of Health and Welfare (AIHW), 1997). This census also noted that a further 1,277 young people under the age of 15 years accessed these services in 1997. It should be noted that there is an overlap between this population and that traditionally served by child welfare authorities, especially as current state wards feature in the SAAP population. Through access to SAAP accommodation services, that are less controlled than child care services used by the majority population, some of Australia most vulnerable young people are encouraged to declare independence and remove themselves from family, school, and other parts of mainstream society. This happens regardless of the fact that legally they are the responsibility of state and territory child welfare authorities. Independence at a young age, for example at 13 or 14 or even 16 years of age, is significantly lower than is usual for even the most well prepared young people (Ainsworth, 1998).

It also needs to be noted that state and territory departments responsible for child welfare services are increasingly contracting out services. For example, in 1996 the New South Wales Community Services department put out to tender 15 intensive accommodation and support services for adolescents. These services, now offered by a range of nongovernment, not-for-profit organizations on a fee-for-service basis, had previously been provided directly by the state department. This is a pattern that is increasingly evident in other states and territories.

Something also needs to be said about the use in Australia of the term "foster care." In the U.S., this term is used generically to refer to all forms of out-of-home care. In the U.K. it is used more precisely to refer to family foster care and kinship care, thereby excluding group care. In Australia, the British practice is usually followed, although the AIHW uses the term "living arrangement" for children under care and protection orders. They then report numbers by categories of care, i.e., foster care or residential facility, but do not break down foster care numbers by type, i.e., family foster care or kinship care.

Finally, it is important to make reference to social values. There is noticeable reference in Australia to a "classless" society based on egalitarian values and on everyone getting "a fair go." These values influence social policy thinking at a governmental level and are supportive of the maintenance of income support schemes for the unemployed, disabled, or aged members of the community. The wide public support of a national health care system further emphasizes these values, which are also evident in relation to child welfare services, especially in regard to national government involvement in services for homeless youth and the attempt to build a universal child care service.

While in some quarters these core values are seen to be under attack by an economic rationalist philosophy and efforts by the current Liberal governments to reduce the size of government, they remain very strong. In this respect Australia, regardless of which political party is in office, reflects social values that are closer to those found in the U.K. than those manifested in the more individually focused U.S. culture.

It is also worth highlighting the importance of indigenous or Aboriginal issues. The *Bringing Them Home* report (Human Rights & Equal Opportunities Commission, 1997a) is a reference for this for the Australian context. The report is about children removed from Aboriginal parents by the state child welfare organizations and placed mainly in the care of orphanages or children's homes run by religious groups, as also seen in parallel experiences in the U.K. and the U.S. As noted by Ainsworth (1998, p. 301–302);

> This shameful practice has forever tainted institutional care and other residential programs in the eyes of Aboriginal people, who represent a significant part of the current population who have contact with the child welfare services.

Notes

1. See Maluccio and Anderson (2000) for discussion of future challenges and opportunities confronting child welfare as we move into the 21st century.

2. See American Humane Association et al. (1998) for a comprehensive framework for assessment of outcomes in child welfare services; Pecora et al. (1996) for discussion of guidelines for quality improvement and evaluation; and Smokowsky and Wodarsky (1996) for a concise review of the empirical evidence regarding the effectiveness of child welfare services.

3. The following references include attention to outcome research in child welfare:

U.S.: Downs, Costin, and McFadden (1996); Kluger, Alexander, and Curtis (2000); and Pecora, Whittaker, Maluccio, and Barth (2000).

U.K.: Department of Health (1989a, 1996, and 1998); Hill and Aldgate (1996); and Jackson and Thomas (1999).

Australia: Gardner (2000); Goddard and Carew (1993); and Goddard (1996).

4. Those wishing to learn more about practice and services in England and Wales will find that the several volumes of Guidance issued when the Act was implemented (Department of Health, 1991) are an excellent and highly readable source. The guidance was accompanied by a set of principles for practice (Department of Health, 1989b), which draw heavily on the "practice wisdom" of the past, as well as the research studies commissioned by the Department of Health and summarized in three separate reviews (Department of Health, 1989b and 1995b). Also, the Department of Health has just published another guidance (Department of Health, 2000b), which describes a research-based framework for assessing children in need and their families. The framework covers areas such as the assessment process, analysis and decision-making, and organizational arrangements for supporting effective assessement of children in need. A companion volume (Department of health, 2000c) provides the knowledge base for the above assessment framework, including theory, research findings, and practice experiences pertaining to black children and disabled children and their families.

Chapter 2

Outcome Research on Traditional Services

This section will consider outcome research regarding "traditional" services, including kinship care, family foster care, treatment foster care, residential group care, and adoption.

Kinship Care

From the U.S.

Researchers as well as administrators in the U.S. are beginning to consider the impact of kinship care on child welfare, especially in the light of dramatic increases in the numbers of children placed formally with relatives, particularly in families of color (cf. Anderson et al. 1997). Until recently, "the lack of attention to parenting of children by their grandparents and other kin has been complemented by a similar ignorance of the degree to which child welfare system has turned to kin as an out-of-home care placement resource" (Courtney & Needell 1997, p. 130). For instance, only in recent years has the outcome of kinship care versus nonrelative foster care been examined in terms of the impact on adult functioning of these children (Benedict et al. 1996). This Maryland study involved 214 children who were in care during the period 1984–1988 and who had reached the age of 18 years by 1993–1994. The first set of measures of adult functioning used in this study relates to years of education, employment status, income level, stability of housing, number of prior addresses, and homelessness.

There were no significant differences in the above study between those who had experienced kinship care and those who had been in nonrelative foster care on all of these parameters. The second set of measures comprised physical health, mental/emotional health, life stresses and social support, drug use, and violence. The measures of drug use and violence were the only ones to produce statistically significant results for the two groups. A greater number of those placed with kin reported heroin usage at some time (28%) as compared to the nonrelative group (11%) (p = <.001). A significantly larger kin group (13% compared with 5%) also reported trading sex for drugs (p = <.03). Further analysis of the data to assess potential confounding factors of any association between kinship care and nonrelative care and the first set of measures of adult functioning—high school education, employment status and mental/emotional health—was also undertaken. The results were inconsistent and the researchers concluded that "young people placed with kin and nonrelative care were functioning similarly in their current lives" (Benedict et al. 1996, p. 545) in terms of these outcomes.

In relation to reunification, some evidence suggests that children stay longer in kinship care than in nonrelative foster care. For example, a study in New York State reported:

> Of all first admissions in 1987, nearly 88% of the children whose first placement was in the home of an approved relative were still in care as of September 30, 1989. In contrast, only 40% of the children placed in regular foster homes were still in care. (Wulczyn as cited in Link, 1996, p. 511)

Other studies have shown that the rates of family reunification for children in formal kinship care are actually lower than those from foster care with nonrelatives (Goerge, 1990; Testa, 1992). A further study of 664 children in foster care in New York State also confirmed these findings (Link, 1996). Similarly, other investigators have found that children placed with relatives return to their birth parents "less quickly and are less likely to be adopted than children in nonrelative foster care" (Needell & Gilbert, 1997, p. 96; see also Testa, 1997; Wulczyn & Goerge, 1992). As Needell and Gilbert (1997, p. 93) have underscored, the "lack of appropriate service provision to birth parents and structural problems in the child welfare system . . . no doubt contribute to the low reunification rates." In connection with this issue, in a case study of the development of kinship care policy in Illinois, Gleeson (1996) concluded that welfare reform efforts resulted in downplaying "the need for income support for poor families and financial support of caregivers and their relative children who come to the attention of the problem child welfare system" (p. 444). He pointed to the challenge of "creating a context that supports protection, permanence, child well-being, and familial and cultural continuity for children in state custody, while supporting kinship networks ... " (p. 444).

In a related study involving in-depth interviewing with caseworkers in a public child welfare agency, Gleeson et al. (1997) described the unique problems and needs of children in kinship care and their parents. In particular, over 80% of the biological mothers of the children in kinship foster care were reported to be suffering from substance abuse problems, and most kinship caregivers suffered serious economic hardships. In regard to financial supports, research by Berrick and Needell (2000) suggests that "the payment rates kinship providers receive may have an effect on a variety of outcomes in child welfare," specifically in reducing the rate of reunification and increasing "the overall length of time children remain in the foster care system" (p. 164).

Agathen, O'Donnell and Wells (1999) have developed a set of instruments to measure the quality of kinship foster care, along with a manual guiding their use. The instruments include a caretaker interview, child interview, case record review, and caseworker questionnaire. They have been field tested with African-American, Latino, and white kinship foster families to ensure that they are applicable across racial, ethnic, and cultural groups.

Although there is much that we still can learn about its application and effectiveness, kinship care may be a promising approach for children in need. If provided in a high quality manner with adequate supports to parents, kinship care can offer stable placements that maintain family continuity and promote child well-being. However, its use raises a number of issues in such areas as licensing and other regulatory procedures; administration; payment to relatives as foster parents; and relationships among children, birth parents, and foster parents. In this connection, Hegar and Scannapieco (1999) offer a comprehensive analysis of kinship care, including practice models that build on available research. Gleeson and Hairston (1999) describe the findings of research projects that can help improve kinship care practice, especially in relation to outreach services to children and their families.

From the U.K.

Kinship care has not been as widely used in the U.K. as in some other countries. In England, however, the Children Act 1989 emphasizes that it should be a placement of choice for those who cannot return safely to birth parents. Since enactment of this Act, the numbers in kinship care have increased. Unlike the U.S., in the U.K. adoption by kinship carers is not generally aimed for, and indeed is seen as distorting relationships among child, birth parents, and relatives.

It should be noted that the official figures for "looked after" children do not give an accurate picture of the extent of kinship care, even for children known to social services departments, because of concerns about child care standards, let alone those who do not cross the social services' thresholds. Most children in kinship care do not enter the formal care system, and if financial or emotional support is needed, it is usually provided through the family support arrangements of the Children Act 1989. Some children are formally accommodated with relatives who are paid and supported as foster carers (in 1997 nearly 4,000 out of approximately 52,000—or 8% of all "looked after" children). Relatives are often encouraged to apply for a "Residence Order" so that they take over full responsibility from the local authority and share parental responsibility with the parents. In a recent study of 105 newly identified child protection cases, Brandon et al. (1999) found that kinship care was widely used as a short-term emergency placement, for the provision of regular periods of respite, as a longer-term placement or as a permanent family placement. Most often it is grandparents who provide kinship care, although sometimes aunts and uncles or older siblings are the carers.

There are no evaluations of the outcomes of short-term placements with relatives. Long-term placements with relatives have been found to be more successful for the full range of children than placement with families not previously known to the child. The main sources here are the two studies by Rowe and her colleagues (1984 and 1989) on long-term placement with relatives and Berridge and Cleaver's (1987) study of foster home breakdown. Rowe et al. (1984)

found that 27% of the 200 foster children in placement for at least four years were placed with relatives; they tended to have higher well-being than those with strangers, were on average higher in self-esteem, and had a greater "sense of permanence." A smaller proportion of the children in the Berridge and Cleaver (1987) sample of 189 planned long-term foster placements were placed with relatives (10%), but these authors note a difference between the two sample authorities, with 30% kinship placements in a London Borough and 4% in the county authority. Only two of the 25 kinship placements broke down within a three-year period (8% compared with 38% for the sample as a whole).

The Grandparents' Federation has had an important part to play in stimulating discussion on kinship care, as well as on the continuation of links between the wider family and children in long-term accommodation or adoptive placements. Their "Residence Orders" study (1998) found a reluctance on the part of local authorities to pay the discretionary Residence Order Allowance to grandparents who took on parental responsibility for their young relatives. A study of an advocacy service for grandparents seeking contact or parental responsibility for their grandchildren found a reluctance to assert their rights to a better service because of anxiety that they would make themselves unpopular with the local authorities and thus lose all contact with their grandchildren (Tunnard & Thoburn, 1997).

From Australia

Formalized kinship care is increasingly viewed by Australian child welfare authorities as the option of first choice. For example, the stated aim of the Department of Family and Children's Services (DFCS) in Western Australia is "over the next three years ... to increase the percentage of placements with relatives from 22 percent to 30 percent" (DFCS, 1996, p. 20), while in New South Wales the stated aim of the Department of Community Services (DCS) is to encourage family and kinship placements "as an alternative to placement with carers unknown to the child" (DCS, 1996, p. 16). This aim is to be pursued against a background where such placements have "increased from 983 or 23% of children in out-of-home care in 1991/92 to 2143 or 37% in 1995/96" (DCS, 1996, p. 17).

There are no published studies of kinship care in Australia. In addition, there is an absence of practice literature addressing this issue. Kinship care is not referenced in either of the two most recent child welfare texts (Goddard & Carew, 1993; Goddard, C., 1996). This deficit has recently been partly addressed by the publication of an article on this topic in an Australian social work journal (Ainsworth & Maluccio, 1998). This article primarily cites the U.S. or British research and the indication is that Australian practice is being driven by these materials or, more likely, by purely pragmatic considerations.

In addition, recently a research project entitled "Understanding Kinship Care" has been launched by the New South Wales Association of Childrens' Welfare Agencies.[1] This one-year project, which commenced in 1999, is the first of its type in Australia. The aim is to determine why children at risk are being placed in the care of relatives and the effectiveness of these arrangements. In addition, the study will compare the support and resources provided to kinship placements versus nonrelative foster care. It will also analyze the perceptions of those involved in kinship care, namely, the children themselves, the carers, the birth parents, and the supervising workers.

Family Foster Care

From the U.S.

In a special issue of *Child Welfare* edited by Barbell and Wright (1999), the contributors focus on the theme of accountability in the outcome of services for children in family foster care and their families, with emphasis on:

- using data for planning in family foster care;
- enhancing outcomes through new models of family foster care; and
- promoting child well-being in family foster care.

The authors note the growing importance of outcome accountability in family foster care, as reflected in new data systems; new funding arrangements at the local, state, and national levels; and new calls for evidence regarding the effectiveness of services. As Barbell and Wright (1999, p. 6) indicate, outcome evaluation is crucial, as the foster care system has been increasingly stretched by dramatic increases in the number of families with children in care and the severity of their needs and problems, while the federal government has modified a wide range of policies that place further demands on agencies.

The assessment of outcome in family foster care in the U.S. is problematic and yields mixed results, for various reasons. First, many of the studies focus on generic foster care and do not distinguish among long-term, short-term, emergency foster care, and treatment foster care. Second, much of the available evaluation research was carried out prior to the recent emphasis on permanency planning, or it examined the situations of children who were placed prior to this emphasis. For the most part, such research dealt with children whose personal or family situations were not as dire as those of children currently in the foster care system; consequently, it may not be totally relevant in terms of the contemporary context. Third, foster care populations are dynamic and constantly changing, in response to changing societal conditions (Goerge, 2000).

For these reasons, it is difficult to carry out rigorous research in this area of child welfare. Many of the available studies are characterized by inadequate sampling, lack of control or comparison groups, and imprecise definition of key variables, among other problems. Yet, child welfare practice must go on, enriched as much as possible by research. Despite the obstacles, researchers continue to try to unravel the complexities of out-of-home care, and there have been many investigations in recent years.

Fein (1991) presents an overview of findings from various investigations, focusing on:

- description of populations served by foster care systems,

- examination of the positive and negative results of foster care placements,

- consideration of the beneficial outcomes of foster care for certain youngsters,

- the economic crisis for foster parents, and

- the vulnerability of minority children and their families.

After calling attention to the mixed results of various outcome studies, Fein concludes:

> The outcomes of foster care placements . . . whether measured in terms of children's functioning or their stability and permanency, are dependent on a complex set of interactive factors that present researchers with exquisite problems in design and methodology. Research lags behind changes in policy and practice, and we are rarely clear about the extent to which yesterday's findings are a function of the basic characteristics of children and families or of the idiosyncrasies of the programs of the past. (Fein, 1991, p. 582).

Two early studies explored the functioning of nearly 200 children placed in short-term family foster care. The first focused on children in care under two years (Fein et al., 1983). The second examined 800 children in long-term family foster care, that is for two years or more (Fein et al., 1990). In both of these studies, the children's functioning, based primarily on reports from the foster parents, was assessed in relation to each of the following areas: school functioning, behavioral functioning, emotional and developmental functioning, and family functioning and family adjustment. In the study of short-term foster care, most children were reported by their foster parents to be functioning moderately well in all areas except for school functioning. There were, however, significant variations in functioning, dependent on characteristics such as placement history, age at initial placement, family income, and marital status of the foster parents (Fein et al., 1983, pp. 542-545).

In the study of the long-term family foster care (Fein et al., 1990), an overall assessment of the children's functioning was obtained by summing up their individual scores in each area noted above. As with those children in short-term care, most children were reported by their foster parents to be functioning well. Higher overall functioning scores were obtained for female, black, and non-disabled children and youth. These youngsters were also likely to have spent more time in the current placement and to have had fewer placements. Higher functioning was also associated with youngsters who had more positive feelings about their birth parents and who lived with foster parents who were older, did not want the child to move to another home, and had seen an improvement since the child's placement in their home.

In another study, Fanshel, Finch, and Grundy (1989; 1990) examined the modes of exit from care and adjustment at departure of 585 children who entered and left foster care placement through the Casey Family Program in various western states between 1966 and 1984. On the basis of content analysis of agency case records, the researchers concluded that over half the children had remained in care until emancipation and that they "left care in relatively good conditions" (p. 401). In addition, as also noted in previous investigations (cf. Fanshel & Shinn, 1978), the researchers found that the children's adjustment at exit was significantly correlated with various characteristics of the child and the family prior to placement. For example, it was found that "greater conflict with the biological parent, a greater number of living arrangements before separation from biological parents, and boys' having been physically abused before entry into care presaged poorer conditions at exit" (Fanshel et al., 1989, p. 401).

Other researchers have underscored the substantial damage that results from the tenuous status in which many foster children find themselves. Such status presumably makes it difficult for a child to develop her or his identity, achieve a sense of belonging, establish meaningful relationships with people, and deal successfully with developmental tasks. In a study of children and youths placed through the state, one-third (34%) of a large representative sample were reported to have significant behavior problems, based on results of the Child Behavior Check List (CBCL). As Landsverk and Garland (2000, p. 196) indicate, "The research literature . . . suggests that between one-half and two-thirds of the children entering foster care exhibit behavior or social competency problems warranting mental health services." In addition,

Research studies over the past two decades have firmly established what practitioners have known for considerably longer, namely, that children in foster care represent a high-risk population for maladaptive outcomes, including socioemotional, behavioral, and psychiatric problems warranting mental health treatments. (Landsverk & Garland, 2000, p. 193)

In a small, nonrandom sample of foster care graduates of various ages from the Casey Family Program, young adults reported experiencing problems with substance abuse and employment; however, without a comparison group, it is difficult to reach definitive conclusions (Fanshel et al., 1990). In fact, most follow-up studies of adults who grew up in foster care do not support the conclusion that out-of-home placement is damaging (Maluccio & Fein, 1985). On the whole, these studies "suggest that the initially negative effects of separation and placement in foster care can be counteracted or reduced through the influence of stable foster home placements and strong services to the children and their foster parents and biological parents" (Fein & Maluccio, 1991, p. 64).

Festinger comprehensively examined the views, experiences, and functioning of 277 young adults who had graduated from foster care in New York City and concluded that, in general, they "were not so different from others their age in what they were doing, in the feelings they expressed, and in their hopes for the future" (1983, p. 293-294). Generally positive outcomes for most graduates of foster care were also found in a follow-up study of children served by a well-funded foster care program of a private agency in the Northwest, although a nonrandom sample was used and the follow-up period varied substantially among the young adults (Fanshel et al., 1990).

In another study, Festinger (1994; 1996) described the situation of 210 children returning to their families from foster care and group care facilities in 20 agencies in New York City. The researchers examined, in particular, whether a child's reentry into foster care was associated with certain child, caregiver, and situational factors. She found that nearly 205 of the children reentered foster care within two years. Multivariate analysis showed that lower ratings of caregivers' parenting skills and less social support were the strongest predictors of reentry within 12 months of leaving care (Festinger, 1996, p. 383).

In a synthesis of a range of studies published between 1960 and 1992 on the long-term effects of placement in foster care, McDonald, Allen, Westerfelt and Piliavin (1996, p. 140) concluded:

> Most of the findings are consistent with practice and policy knowledge supporting the use of foster family placements over group or institutional placement and stressing the need for stability. Other findings, however, strongly contradict current thinking in the out-of-home care field—that long-term foster care is harmful to the child.

More recently, Pecora, Kingery, Downs, and Nollan (1997) examined the effectiveness of family foster care, particularly for adolescents, by analyzing existing research in the following outcome areas: chemical dependency, criminal behavior, depression, education, marital status and number of children, and self-sufficiency. These authors reported mixed results and pointed to various methodological limitations and conceptual complexities in the studies that they reviewed, especially the issue of whether the difficulties faced by young people leaving foster care were caused by the placement or were present at the point at which they entered the system due to poverty, family problems, or other conditions. They concluded that, while we know much about child maltreatment and its effects, there is a paucity of rigorously gathered research data and many unexamined questions regarding the long-term effects of placement, and how foster care might help protect young people from further maltreatment and overcome its effects.

Pecora et al. (1998) also reported on an outcome survey of 312 youths between the ages of 16 and 19 (184 male, 128 female; 164 children of color, 87 multiethnic) served by the Casey Family Program. The average time these youths had spent with Casey was 4.8 years and the average time in their current placement was 4.6 years. Eight areas of personal functioning were examined, with the following results:

- Emotional functioning (e.g., self esteem was good, and a sense of hope was present in 90% of youths).

- Placement stability, in terms of the number of disruptions while with Casey (e.g., 51.5% of the youths had only one placement, 69.7% had two or less placements).

- Some areas of cultural identity development (e.g., sense of ethnic identity was generally good, respect for elders was rated as present).

- Usage of tobacco products (e.g., only 14% of the youths in the sample smoke one cigarette or more every day).

- Educational competence (e.g., school attendance, reading activity, grade point average, and average grade levels in certain subject areas were comparable to the general population).

- Volunteer or paid employment experience for youths (e.g., 95% had worked during summer or school breaks, 21.8% had volunteer experience).

- Illegal behavior (e.g., low rates of status offences and felonies).

This study provides encouraging data about the outcomes of services such as those provided by the Casey Family Program. When considering these results, it is important to note that this agency offers one of the exemplar U.S. foster care programs.

Other investigators have called attention to the plight of the increasing numbers of very young children in foster care. As Kemp and Bodonyi (2000) point out, there has been little empirical attention "to the sizable group of these children who are not reunited with their biological families and who then remain in care for long periods" (p. 95). In a descriptive study of 458 legally free children who entered foster care as infants, Kemp and Bodonyi (2000) examined length of stay and permanency outcomes. They found that long stays in care were the norm and that few were either reunited with their families or readily placed in permanent homes. In particular, black children were less likely to achieve permanence than white children. The study suggested "the need for flexible approaches to permanency . . . and for attention to children's long-term developmental needs as well as to strategies that better assure placement stability" (p. 95).

In an integrative review of their studies as well as the work of other researchers, Berrick et al. (1998) point to the poor outcomes of child welfare services for these children, whose specialized needs are not adequately considered in a child welfare system that has traditionally focused on school-age children and on undifferentiated services. Building on their research, they offer a comprehensive set of recommendations for transforming child welfare practice for young children, through emphasis on timely decision-making; recognizing through law the differential needs of these children; promoting developmentally sensitive child welfare practice; and incorporating greater emphasis on promotion of child well-being.

Finally, others have focused on the phenomenon of breakdown of foster home placement. In a review of related research from Australia, the U.S., and the U.K., Berridge and Cleaver (1987) indicated that breakdown rates were as high as 50% of the placements. In the U.S., Fein et al. (1983) found that 50% of the children placed in permanent foster care experienced disruption of their placement within one-and-a-half years. However, this was a very small sample of 14 children, most of whom were teenagers. In the comprehensive study of the Casey Family Program mentioned earlier (Fanshel et al., 1989), which involved nearly 600 children, 24.6% of the placements had apparently failed, as the children ran away or were returned to the courts. Also, approximately 50% had more than one Casey placement. In a more recent study in another community, it was found that nearly half of the children who entered foster care prior to the age of six (and remained for at least four years) had three or more foster care placements during their stay (Needell et al., 1998).

As reflected in the above review, research on the functioning of children during or after placement has not led to consistent or definitive findings that can clearly guide policy and practice. As noted, most of these studies have methodological limitations, such as small samples, lack of comparison groups, biased sampling, limited outcome measures, and retrospective data collection. Moreover, it is becoming increasingly apparent that "the outcome of foster care placement, whether measured in terms of children's functioning or stability or permanency, depends on a complex set of factors that are 'interactive' and difficult to measure" (Fein et al., 1990, p. 76). At the same time, "we must recognize the complexity of human beings and that the instruments that measure functioning and the policies that guide interventions only approximate the complexities . . . when applied to individuals" (Fein & Maluccio, 1992, p. 345). In addition, we should note that the face of family foster care in the next few decades may be substantially altered by such factors as welfare reform, increasing reliance on kinship networks, and changing demographics including substantial increases in the numbers of children of color (Courtney & Maluccio, 2000). As Traglia et al. (1997) argue, outcome-oriented case planning will be essential in family foster care.[2]

From the U.K.

Kelly and Gilligan (2000) assess the current state of foster care in the U.K., including the challenges it faces. There is a long tradition of researching family foster care in the U.K., much of it independently conducted but funded by the Department of Health. However, until fairly recently, outcome research has been less helpful than it might otherwise be because of the inclusion in a single study of foster placements with very different aims. There is no clear distinction in many studies between "foster family care" and "treatment foster care" (see next section), and there is some overlap between studies of "permanent" foster care and adoption. A survey by Waterhouse (1996) of fostering arrangements concluded that most local authorities had specialist schemes, but these provided only a small proportion of the total number of placements. The major resource was still the "traditional" foster family, providing homes for a range of children from a day to a lifetime. Although the literature on foster care is extensive, that which specifically considers outcomes for the children is fairly limited. It will be examined here under the broad categories of short-term or task-centered family foster care; longer-term placement; and placements intended to provide a "family for life."

Triseliotis, Borland, and Hill (2000) provide a rich picture of the fostering careers and attitudes of 835 Scottish foster parents (a 74% sample of the 1132 families to whom a postal questionnaire was sent). There are no outcome data on the children, but two particularly informative chapters provide data on the 753 children for whom foster placements had been sought during a six-week period, and the reasons why 149 foster carers ceased to foster. The main reason most often cited (by 26%) was dissatisfaction with the foster care services, though it must be said that foster carers did not give up easily since, on average, they had been looking after foster children for 7.5 years.

Another study of foster parents found that certain qualities of social workers played a substantial role in the retention of foster homes and in the satisfaction and commitment of foster carers (Fisher et al., 2000). These qualities included, in particular: ability to listen and offer encouragement, ready availability and response to foster parents, keeping foster carers informed and included in planning, and ensuring prompt processing of payments, complaints, and recommendations for change.

In other publications, Berridge (1997), Jackson and Thomas (1999), Sellick and Thoburn (1996), and Triseliotis, Sellick, and Short (1995) summarize the research on the outcomes of the different types of foster care. Jackson and Thomas (1999) focus on studies examining practice that is effective in creating stability for children in care. Also of importance are statistics produced annually by the Department of Health, *Children Looked After by Local Authorities*; the latest edition shows that on March 31, 1997, over 28,000 of the 51,600 children looked after by local authorities were placed in foster family care; a further 4,000 were placed as foster children with relatives, and around 6,000 experienced a series of short periods in the same respite foster family during the year (Department of Health, 1998). Sellick and Thoburn (1996) identify the range of outcome measures that may be used to evaluate success in foster care and also the difficulties inherent in identifying reasons for more successful or less successful placements when so many variables about the children, parents, and social work practice are interacting.

The work of Jane Rowe has been of central importance in elucidating the aims of foster care and devising outcome measures appropriate to the different groups of children being placed (Rowe et al., 1989). This study of placements made by six Social Service Departments included 3,796 foster family placements. It concluded that placements aiming to provide temporary care were most likely to succeed (88% successful). Emergency placements (83% successful) and preparation for long-term placement (79% successful) also generally had positive outcomes. However, placements aiming to provide assessment (57% successful), treatment (46% successful), and bridge to independence (53% successful) had more difficulty in achieving their aims.

Most other studies use breakdown of placement as the major outcome measure. There have been few British studies of short-term foster family placements and of those available, more research time has been spent on specialist task-centered foster family placement for adolescents. Berridge and Cleaver (1987) combined a scrutiny of records on all foster family placements made by two contrasting local authorities and a voluntary child care agency with qualitative interviews with each participant in 10 cases which broke down. They found that only 10% of 156 planned short-term foster placements ended prematurely, but that a more serious problem was that some children stayed longer than planned (28%). These authors reported that the reasons for breakdown identified in social work records were "child focused" in 30% of cases; foster-family focused in 37% of cases; and jointly child and foster-family focused in 23% of cases. In only 3% of the cases was the behavior of birth parents seen as part of the reason for breakdown. On the contrary, placements were more likely to fail when parental access was restricted by the agency.

Sellick (1992) took up the theme of placement-related factors contributing to stability in a qualitative exploration of the support needs of 18 short-term foster carers recruited by six statutory and two voluntary sector agencies. He concluded that the range of support needs came under the headings: professional support from their "own" family placement worker and the child's worker; mutual support from other foster carers; respite care; financial and

practical (e.g., insurance against breakages); and a "mixed diet"—
what in the U.S. might be referred to as "wraparound" services.

Aldgate and Bradley (1999) described 13 respite care schemes
for families under stress and followed the experiences of 60 children
through a period of respite care. Using a range of outcome measures,
including the satisfaction of the parents, children, and carers, they
found that the outcomes were generally positive. Numbers were too
small for statistical testing of associations between child, family, and
placement variables and outcomes. However, the conclusions point
toward a model of social work practice that involves continuity of
relationship with the social worker for the carers, children, and
parents alongside a range of family support services. Similar results
have been found with respect to children with disabilities by Robinson
(1987) and Stalker (1990).

Intermediate length or long-term foster care have had important parts to play in child placement policy and practice, despite
being generally frowned upon in a climate much influenced by the
American "permanence" movement, which led to a preference for
restoration to the birth family or adoption. Berridge and Cleaver
(1987) included 150 long-term foster placements in their study of
foster care breakdown. Forty-eight percent in one authority but only
29% in the other broke down within five years. As with short-term
placements, the major reasons for breakdown, as identified in social
work records, were "placement-focused" (30%); "child-focused"
(20%); or "placement and child-focused" (37%). The behavior of
natural parents was included in the reasons for breakdown in only
8% of cases. Included in "placement-focused" reasons were marital
problems and other relationship difficulties within the foster family.
In this, as in other studies, having a child close in age to the placed
child was associated with breakdown.

Aldgate, Colton, Ghate, and Heath (1992) focused on the educational attainment of 49 children aged 8–14 who had been in local
authority care for at least six months. Most had been in the same
placement for much longer, the median stay being seven years. The
children were compared with a group of 58 children who came from
similar backgrounds and were receiving social work support ser-

vices in their own homes. Standardized tests in reading, vocabulary, and mathematics were used and repeated after 12 months. The educational attainment of the foster children compared unfavorably with children in the general population but was similar to the comparison group. Regression analysis was used to tease out differences among the foster children in terms of their educational scores and progress. Those whose placements were planned to be long-term from the start were doing better (regression coefficient significant at .01 level) as were those whose placements had lasted longer and who came into care for reasons other than abuse or neglect.

Schofield, Beek, and Sargent (2000) reported on the first stage of a longitudinal study of 58 children who were placed in foster care with the intention at the time of placement that it would be a long-term arrangement, or the majority, whose short-term foster placements had been recently confirmed as long-term. In the first report, data from interviews with parents, social workers, and carers were used to describe the circumstances of the young people and their patterns of attachment with carers and birth relatives. It was found that long-term foster care was the placement of choice for many older children who have histories of maltreatment and are not likely to be able to return for the foreseeable future to birth parents or relatives. For most, there was a clear recorded plan that the children would remain with the same foster families throughout childhood. In spite of anxieties expressed in the literature that long-term foster placements remain legally and procedurally insecure, most of the skilled carers were able to build secure attachment relationships. The researchers pose the question, which they will follow up in the next round of interviews, as to whether this important relationship-building and therapeutic process would be enhanced if there were increased legal and procedural safeguards.

Thoburn (1991) differentiated between "long-term" foster placements where the planned length of stay was uncertain at the time of placement, and "permanent" placements which were made with the intention that the child would remain indefinitely with that same family. From a survey of 1,165 adoptive or permanent foster family placements with "stranger" families made by British voluntary child care agencies between 1980 and 1986, she concluded that there was no difference in breakdown rates between children placed permanently with foster families and those placed for adoption, once age at placement was controlled for (Thoburn, 1991). On the same theme, Gibbons et al. (1995) found that children maltreated when under age five and placed in long-term foster care were, on average, doing as well as similar children who had been adopted and those who returned to or remained with parents.

Another variable that has received attention is that of ethnicity of the children to be placed and of the parents. From a more recent study of a subgroup of 297 children of minority ethnic origin (around a third of whom were placed in "permanent" foster family care and two-thirds of whom were placed for adoption), Thoburn, Norford, and Rashid (2000) concluded that breakdown rates were similar for children of minority ethnic origin to those for white children, and that those placed in ethnically matched families were as likely as those placed transracially to experience breakdown. They found that children of minority ethnic origin were more likely than white children to be placed in long-term or permanent foster care and white children more likely to be placed for adoption. From the qualitative data, it appears that this is in part explained by the fact that black and Asian substitute parents tend to come from lower socioeconomic backgrounds and are therefore in greater need of the fostering allowance, but also that they were culturally more attuned to finding rewards in helping black children and their parents through long-term arrangements that did not sever the legal links between the child and the birth family. Most of the above studies mention sibling placements, and most researchers and practitioners conclude that siblings should not be placed separately without good cause.

Several studies have considered the child-related, birth family-related and foster family-related variables associated with better or worse outcomes, but numbers are often too small to reach reliable conclusions about associations between outcome and these variables. Cleaver (2000) used social work records to study the family contact provisions of the Children Act 1989 in respect of 162 foster care placements of at least three months duration made by six local authorities. The cases were followed up four years later and there was a prospective intensive interview sample of 33 children aged between 5 and 12 at the time of placement. When compared with the earlier sample of Berridge and Cleaver (1987), it was found that those who had some family contact were, in the post-Children Act period, more likely to see parents and other relatives more frequently. Some 40% saw a birth parent at least once a week (45% for those who stayed less than a year, and 33% for placements lasting more than a year). However, a third of those in placement for less than a year and 40% in placement for over a year had no contact with either parent. In line with previous studies, the frequency of contact was associated with return home. Contact with the mother was also associated with the child's "adequate adjustment" to the foster home (83.5% adequately adjusted if they had contact and 66.7% if they did not ($x2(1) = 4.65$; $p<.05$). Although focusing on contact, this detailed study contains important information about other aspects of foster care.

To sum up, despite frequently voiced criticisms, short, respite and long-term foster family care represents the mainstay of British child placement practice (Thoburn, 1990, 1999). Although long-term foster care has fallen into disrepute in official circles and child welfare texts, it is still also very widely used and outcomes are generally as positive as the alternatives for each age range. As seen in a study of the perspectives of children in Northern Ireland aged four and eleven (McCauley, 1996), the positive outcome of such care can be promoted through continuity in the child relationships with birth families, better preparation for foster placements, and greater coordination with the child's former school and other community agencies.[3]

From Australia

Family foster care research in Australia is limited. Studies have examined the recruitment of foster carers (Keogh & Svensson, 1999; Vollard et al., 1993); the induction practices of foster care agencies (Dyer & Evans, 1997); the qualities required to be a foster carer (Juratowich & Smith, 1996); and the characteristics of foster care families (Evans & Tierney, 1995). The most recent study of the recruitment of foster carers in Melbourne indicates that only 4% of families who responded to a foster care publicity campaign actually became foster carers (Keogh & Svensson, 1999). There is also an investigation of foster care drift in Western Australia (McCotter & Oxnam, 1981), with inconclusive findings. Another study in New South Wales (Fernandez, 1996) examined the factors that influenced the placement careers of children admitted to substitute care for protection purposes. This study described how certain variables, especially time in care and multiple placements, result in a declining rate of reunification. Another study of state wards leaving care (Cashmore & Paxman, 1996), which is described in a later section on preparation for independent living, concluded that the young people were poorly prepared for leaving care. Finally, an unpublished Master's degree thesis also examines the experience of young people leaving care in Queensland (Wilson, 1997). These studies to a large extent replicate the findings of earlier studies undertaken in the U.K. in relation to the same issues (Millham et al., 1986; Stein & Carey, 1986).

In another study, Delfabbro, Barber, and Cooper (2000) examined the extent of disruption experienced by 235 children between the ages of 4 and 17 who were placed in substitute care in South Australia in 1998–1999. Key measures of disruption were: frequency of placement changes, the number of children forced to change school, the geographic distance from birth parents, and the amount of planned contact between the child and their family during placement. It was found that parental contact was reduced when children were abused but more common when children were placed because of parental incapacity. Changes in school were more likely (43%) when children were older or were placed a long way from their families. As expected, geographic dislocation was more likely to be a feature of rural placements, although there were no rural-metropolitan differences in the nature and frequency of family contact. Implications for research included use of a prospective longitudinal design, which is "likely to provide greater insights into the relative importance of placement experiences in the development and well-being of children in care (Delfabbro, Barber, & Cooper, 2000, p. 20).

Other research reports may have been completed by state and territory child welfare authorities. Unfortunately, where they do exist, these reports generally have limited circulation. This research deficit is further emphasized by the fact that the section on family foster care in Goddard and Carew's (1993) Australian text on child welfare almost exclusively cites British and American sources. This limited research on family foster care in Australia may of course be associated with the low number of children in foster care (14,667 in family foster care, kinship care, and group care in 1995–1996) (Moyle & Gibson, 1997). This lack of local research does mean that child welfare personnel are forced to draw on research developed in a cultural climate that is different from Australia. In addition, the influences of cultural factors reported results may not be fully understood by local practitioners.

Treatment Foster Care

From the U.S.

Treatment foster care, also labeled therapeutic foster care or specialized foster care, has been defined as "a model of care and treatment [developed] to meet the needs of children who require the structure that characterizes an institutional program but who could benefit from the richness and normalizing influence of a family environment" (Bryant & Snodgrass, 1990, p. 1). Its goal "is to promote permanence, stability, and family continuity for children [with serious emotional behavioral problems] through individualized, strength-based services" (Thomlison, 1995, p. 195). As defined by the Foster Family-based Treatment Association (1995, p. 6):

> A Treatment Foster Care Program is a family-based service delivery approach providing individualized treatment for children, youth and their families. Treatment is delivered through an integrated constellation of services, with key intervention and supports provided by treatment foster parents who are trained, supervised and supported by qualified program staff.

In line with the above definition, there is general agreement that treatment foster care refers to the provision of family foster care that encompasses characteristics such as the following:

- systematic evaluation and selection of prospective foster parents;

- view of foster care as a goal-oriented service;

- adequate compensation, benefits, and rewards for foster parents based on training, experience, merit, and job expectations;

- training for foster parents on a continuing basis, including incentives for completion of training programs;

- careful matching of foster parents with the kinds of children whom they can most effectively help;

- participation of foster parents as members of the agency's service team;

- provision of supports to foster parents, such as quick access to social workers; and

- involvement of foster parents in helping birth parents (Hudson & Galaway, 1989; Meadowcroft & Trout, 1990; Thomlison, 1995).

Despite the growing acceptance of treatment foster care at the philosophical level, in the U.S., professional foster parenting is far from being implemented in practice and not all "treatment" foster parents are professionalized. However, there are some exemplary programs, such as PRYDE in Pennsylvania, Boystown in Nebraska, and People's Places in Virginia (Hawkins & Breiling, 1989; Meadowcroft & Trout, 1990), and The Casey Family Program, based in Seattle (Massinga & Perry, 1994). The greatest obstacle to the professionalization of family foster care undoubtedly involves insufficient fiscal resources, particularly in public agencies, for adequate compensation of foster parents, reasonable worker caseloads, respite care, and other support services. There has been discussion of—but little movement toward—payment of appropriate salary with full benefits for professional foster parents. Additional barriers include insufficient clarity in respect to the differential roles of foster parents and social workers, the limited training of most foster parents, and the natural inertia produced by any call for large-scale institutional change. There is also a serious shortage of foster parents who are willing and qualified to work with the expanding population of children and youths requiring specialized care and treatment. In the face of expanding need, recruitment and retention of foster parents are becoming increasingly difficult.

Despite its growing use, there has been limited research on effectiveness of treatment foster care. However, agencies that have been able to implement professional foster parenting, generally voluntary agencies providing therapeutic foster care, report good results in terms of success in helping children and youths with serious emotional or behavioral problems (Gore, 1994; Hawkins & Breiling, 1989; Meadowcroft & Trout, 1990).

In a study conducted in the state of Illinois, Testa and Rolock (1999) compared the effectiveness of professional foster care with trained, professional foster parents who were paid an annual salary versus traditional foster care services for children with special needs such as emotional or health problems. These authors found that professional foster care "consistently outperformed" the other programs "in terms of stability, sibling placement, restrictiveness of care, and proximity to the child's community of origin (Testa & Rolock, 1999, p. 108).

In light of the growing shortage of qualified foster parents, it is imperative that further attention be given to issues involved in professionalization of foster parents, especially issues of compensation, training and professional development, supports and rewards, and role clarification. Moreover, although not everyone agrees that all foster parents should be treated as professionals, there is growing consensus that the professionalization of at least some foster parents is an idea whose time has come. But there is an urgent need for national leadership—to explore this idea and its implications, to examine exemplary programs and strategies and their components, to formulate pertinent policies and procedures, and to conduct evaluative research.

From the U.K.

As already noted, there is an overlap between "traditional" foster care and treatment foster care. Indeed, although much of the foster care literature is about "treatment foster care," Rowe et al. (1989) found that only 3% of all teenagers being fostered were in placements specifically designated as "treatment" or "specialist." These schemes started to be developed in the early 1980s, when Nancy Hazel (1981) set up a professional fostering scheme for adolescents along the lines being used in Sweden. Schemes for children with disabilities quickly followed, mainly provided by voluntary child care agencies such as Barnardos (Ames Reed, 1993, 1996/97). Hazel and Fenyo (1993) completed a longer-term evaluation of the Kent foster care scheme initiated by Hazel and concluded that there was general satisfaction in the long-term as well as the short-term. Shaw and Hipgrave (1983 and 1989) described specialist schemes after completing a survey of 45 of them in local authorities and voluntary organizations. Their study, which encompassed an evaluation of a pilot project in one authority, concluded with Hazel that satisfaction of the young people and the carers was generally high but that there was still considerable movement with many placements ending earlier than planned.

The work of Shaw and Hipgrave (1983), Hazel (1990), and Hill et al. (1993) indicates that young people involved in specialist schemes generally expressed satisfaction with the help they received, but rates of unplanned movement for all teenagers appeared to be high. For example, Rowe et al. (1989) found that results were poorer for adolescents than for younger children: in 48% of the placements of children aged 11 or over, "treatment" did not last for as long as needed, compared with 27% of those aged between 5 and 10, and 28% of those under 5. Indeed, when placements of adolescents in foster care were compared with placements of similar aged children in residential care, findings on outcome were broadly comparable (Rowe et al., 1989). These authors also noted that "overstaying" is a problem, although it is debatable as to whether this is a problem for the authorities or for the young people. Shaw and Hipgrave (1989) reported that families felt under pressure to push the children out into independence earlier than necessary and that they and the social workers had a sense of failure if the young people wished to stay on. One might conclude that these are successful placements from the point of view of the young people, though it is problematic for the agency to have to recruit additional specialist carers if there are no longer vacancies within the families.

Caesar et al. (1994) describe a "professional permanence" scheme that encourages specialist foster parents caring for some of the most disturbed young people to continue to care for them as they move into adult life. The study focused on young people of minority ethnic origin and found a high success rate in placing these young people, some of whom had previously been living in youth treatment centers for children who had committed serious criminal offenses or been uncontrollable in more open place-ments. The numbers in the study were small, but the detailed evaluations of well-being and social and cultural identity merit careful study and replication in larger scale work.

Thoburn's (1994) overview of child placement in the U.K. iden-tified an overlap between small group care placements and larger foster homes caring for children in nontypical family situations. Changes in legislation now require these to register as small children's homes, but they have many of the features of foster family care. Perhaps the best known scheme is the Children's Family Trust, which establishes foster carers in homes for groups of children where they remain until the children have grown up. Evaluations are positive in terms of stability of placements and continuing contact with members of the birth families. Cairns (1984) found a breakdown rate of less than 8% within five years of placement.

Colton (1988) used a qualitative/ethnographic method to study in detail 12 "specialist" foster homes (with 40 children) and 12 children's homes (involving 147 children). All except three of the children were aged 12 or over. He found that there was no difference in breakdown rates, and that both groups made similar progress in relation to physical violence, truancy, delinquency, and behavior problems at school and educational performance. However, from his interviews with the young people and their carers, he concluded that foster homes tended to be more child-centered and to have better contacts with the community.

Farmer and Pollock (1998) included children placed in treatment foster care among their sample of abused and abusing children. This study is described more fully in the section on residential care, but has important implications for an understanding of foster care outcomes, since increasing numbers of children placed with foster families have been sexually abused or have come into care because they have sexually abused another child.

From Australia

Formal treatment foster care schemes have not been fully developed in Australia. However, many children in family foster care are receiving specialist assistance with emotional, behavioral, and educational issues. A limited numbers of schemes do exist, such as Barnardos in New South Wales, MacKillop Family Services in Victoria, and the Department of Family and Children's Services in Western Australia. In these situations, specialist foster carers are recruited for especially troubled children, but these schemes are not necessarily referred to as "treatment" foster care.

A recently submitted Masters thesis examines a "specialist home based care" service provided by MacKillop Family Services from the perspective of the foster carers and social workers (Moore, 1999). This qualitative study is of six foster carers and the four workers involved with the service. It seeks to identify the factors that contribute to a successful placement. However, this study does not measure the gains young people have made while in a specialist placement, and success is defined in terms of placement continuity.

The limited number of treatment foster care schemes may reflect Australian values, which place a greater emphasis on structural issues such as poverty as a factor influencing troublesome behaviors than on theories of individual maladjustment as may be the case in the U.S. (Ainsworth, 1997).

Residential Group Care

From the U.S.

An extensive study by the U.S. General Accounting Office concluded the following:

> Not enough is known about residential care programs to provide a clear picture of which kind of treatment approaches work best or about effectiveness of the treatment over the long term. Further, no consensus exists on which youths are best served in residential care . . . or how residential care should be combined with community based care to serve at-risk youth over time. (U.S. General Accounting Office, 1994, p. 4)

The use of residential treatment continues to be controversial, with some authors arguing that "there is little evidence of the effectiveness of residential treatment, especially relative to well conceptualized nonresidential alternatives, but the primary problem of residential treatment may be avoiding negative effects" (Melton et al., 1998, p. 47). Other scholars present a more balanced picture of the role of residential treatment and point to priorities for future research, notably in respect to the impact of community and familial factors in the post-discharge environment (Whittaker & Pfeiffer, 1994). After examining its research base, Whittaker (2000a) offers suggestions for rethinking the role of residential treatment within the continuum of child and family welfare services. In a related article, Whittaker (2000b) identifies various challenges for research in residential treatment, including residential program design and definition, assessment and intake, community aftercare, and outcomes. He underscores the need to study developmental outcomes for youth in residential care through longitudinal research.

Research into the effectiveness of residential group care programs has begun to produce results that deserve some attention. The most rigorous large-scale empirical outcome study in child welfare to date in the U.S. was carried out by Fanshel, Finch, and Grundy (1990). This study is of 585 children in the care of the Casey Family

Program in five western states. It was a retrospective, longitudinal study based on archival data. In the context of the study, the researchers hypothesized that a group care placement would be associated with some positive therapeutic benefit for the child. Such a placement was used at least once in 21.1% of the 585 cases. Multivariate analysis techniques were used to test for associations between the use of a group care placement and the child's condition at exit from care. The study found that a child who had a group care placement while in the Casey program was in better condition at exit from group care (p<.001). This was especially strong for children who adapted poorly while in Casey care (p<.001). Accordingly, the researchers reported that when well planned, positive benefits flow to the children from group care placements.

There is an equally impressive study of youth and family characteristics and treatment histories at Boysville, which is a large residential facility for delinquent adolescents (Whittaker et al., 1990). These researchers found favorable placement outcomes in a study of 239 youths released from the Clinton, Michigan, campus of Boysville. Using the data relating to the youth's release status and defining "planned release" as a measure of outcome, it was possible to examine the relationship between a series of family and youth treatment process variables and intake characteristics. On average, those who stayed in the program longer (14.1 vs. 8.7 months, p<.001), had twice the family worker face-to-face contact (12.1 vs. 6.1, p<.001), received significantly more family work by staff (1047 vs. 485 minutes, p<.001), and had higher total family contact, including telephone, (20.7 vs. 11.8, p = .002). In addition, success related to a number of intake variables. These included age at admission, the number of prior adjudications (2.0 vs. 1.7, p = .03) and the living situation prior to entering Boysville.

Boysville has also completed a longitudinal study of adult imprisonment in Michigan of male youths released from their group homes and campus residential facilities between 1985 and 1987 (Kapp et al., 1994). The cohorts for 1985 were followed for five years and for 1987 for three years. These results show that of the 242 youths released in 1985, 75%, or 184, were not subject to imprisonment in the five years to 1990. For the 1987 cohort of 317, an even larger percentage, 80%, or 255, avoided imprisonment in the three years to 1990. Multivariate analysis was then used to construct a predictive model of adult imprisonment. The risk factors identified as associated with increased odds of imprisonment were: race (white vs. nonwhite), number of adjudications prior to placement (juvenile offender vs. nonoffender), and venue at discharge (home setting vs. nonhome). The most at-risk group were nonwhite youths with prior offenses who did not return home at discharge. Expressed in terms of differential odds of imprisonment,

> The odds are almost one in five (18/100) that these youths will graduate into . . . the adult prison system. The odds of being imprisoned were virtually double those of nonwhite juvenile offenders who returned home. Least vulnerable were white non juvenile offenders who returned home on discharge. They are 4.5 times less likely to find themselves in the adult prison system than the vulnerable group. (Kapp et al., 1994, p. 29)

This study clearly highlights the positive value of home placement for youth with offense histories and the importance of removing barriers to family reunification that may exist in group care settings (Petr & Entriken, 1995).

There is also a fine ethnographic study of the Rochester Jewish Children's Home that involved interviewing former residents now in their later adult years about their lifetime achievements (Goldstein, 1996). This study, together with others (Maunders, 1994; Weiner & Weiner, 1990; Zmora, 1994), suggests that the commonly held view that "group care (programs) for children and youth are counterproductive and even intrinsically abusive . . . and [the view that] programs always have a negative effect may be wrong" (Beker, 1996, p. 214). As Beker also indicates, "reports of happy memories and good outcomes among adults who were raised in group care are not unusual, not merely the exception that many claim them to be" (Beker, 1996, p. 214).

Even more impressively, McKenzie (1997, 1998), in reporting on how well 1,600 alumni of nine orphanages in the U.S. South and

Midwest have done in later life, provides evidence that these individuals were more successful than their counterparts in the general population. That is, those from the orphanages outpaced their counterparts on measures of education, income, and attitude toward life. It should be noted, however that the above studies in general refer to institutional programs going back several decades and may therefore have limited relevance for the population of youths currently going into residential care.[4]

From the U.K.

The British research on group care tends to describe the characteristics of residents, social work, and group care processes, and ,less often, outcomes for cohorts of children placed in several residential units rather than evaluating specific treatment programs, as is more often the case in U.S. There is an overlap between the outcome research on small children's homes and on treatment foster care. At the other end of the continuum, boarding schools used by general populations of British children, as well as those for children with special educational needs, provide care and education for substantial numbers of children in care (Grimshaw & Berridge, 1994; Bullock, 1999). The most striking information on group care in the U.K. is revealed by the annual Department of Health statistics, which show a fall of 47% between 1971 and 1991 in the number of children under 18 living in residential establishments. Fewer than 14,000 of the children in the care of local authorities (around a quarter of the total of 54,000) are in group care settings. However, as Rowe et al. (1989) point out in their study of over 9,000 placements of children in care, many more children "pass through" children's homes as emergency placements when they leave home, or when one foster or adoptive placement has broken down and while they wait for another one to be identified.

The place of residential care in the British child care system is mapped out most recently by the Department of Health (1998) review of 12 research studies. The studies used different methodologies, and involved small-scale qualitative studies of process and larger scale outcome studies. Collectively, they provide information on over 1,300 children who lived, fairly recently, in around 200 group care establishments. Berridge and Brodie (1998) found that children's homes are used mainly as a short or intermediate length placement for younger children; to provide respite and some long-term care for children with disabilities; to prepare adolescents for independent living; and (mainly in the independent sector) to provide long-term care, often also with education on site. Collectively the studies show that most young people enter group care when over the age of 11, following conflict with their parents or foster parents, often exacerbated by their own difficult behavior and by the experience of physical or sexual abuse, or neglect.

Utting (1991) concluded from his review of residential care in England, which followed a series of child abuse scandals, that there was still an important place for group care. Mostly he saw this in terms of short-term placement, "bridge" placement, or preparation for independent living, but he also argued that there is the need for some children to be placed in longer-term group care situations, especially if they have been severely harmed or express a preference for group care over foster care. Fletcher's (1993) survey of young people in care leads her to a similar conclusion.

Turning to outcome studies, as with foster care, group care outcomes need to be assessed in the context of the aims of the placement. Rowe et al. (1989) and Colton (1988) found similar breakdown rates for placements in group care and foster family care when variables such as age at placement were held constant. Rowe et al. (1989) rated 46% of 1,859 placements in group care as "successful" and 16% as "unsuccessful," with the remainder having mixed outcomes. In line with Colton (1988) and Milham et al. (1986), they conclude that outcomes for children of similar ages in residential care compare well with outcomes for foster care placements. In Rowe's study, only 13% of residential placements failed to last as long as needed for those under 11 at placement and 22% of those over 11 at placement. This compares with 20% and 38% for foster placements, though this finding is influenced by the fact that planned long-term placement in residential care is less frequent. On the other hand, Rutter and Giller (1983) found that the parenting abilities of 81 mothers who as children had spent lengthy periods in residential group care were lower than those of a group of mothers living in similar circumstances who had not been in care. Triseliotis and Russell (1984) found that 55% of 40 young adults brought up mainly in residential care were "positive" or "fairly positive" about the experience, as compared with 82% of 44 adults placed for adoption when past infancy. Rose (1990) reviews the work of the Peper Harrow Trust, but this account is more descriptive than evaluative and concerns processes rather than outcomes. Two Department of Health commissioned overviews of research on older children within the care system (Department of Health, 1996, 1998) summarize much of the research on residential care. Triseliotis et al. (1995) give details of children in group care in their study of social work with adolescents.

All recent British studies have found that increasing numbers of those in both residential and foster care have been sexually abused. In a study which crosses over residential and foster care, Farmer and Pollock (1998) scrutinize the care files (approximately 12 months after the start of the latest care episode) of 154 children who were not believed to be either sexually abusive or to have been sexually abused with 89 who had been sexually abused (or suspected as having been); and 24 who were known or suspected as having been sexually abusive. There was overlap between the "abuse" groups so that the total numbers of files studied was 250. The mean age for the "abuse" group was 10.8 and that for the "non-abuse" group was 8. Sixty-three percent of the "abuse" group and 69% of the others were initially placed in foster family care but all "moved frequently between placements within the care system" (p. 41), with 17% moving between different "types" of placement. A subsample of 38 children from the "abuse" group, who were all over the age of 10 at time of placement, were interviewed, as were their carers and social workers (17 abused, 17 victim/perpetrators, and four perpetrators).

The above study provides detailed information on the backgrounds and early care histories of the young people as well as on the carers' biographies and training, on therapeutic interventions and processes, and on satisfaction. For those in the interview sample, outcome data between six and 12-plus months after joining the "index" placement are provided. A particular focus was on the sexual and sexualized behavior of the young people within and outside the placement and on whether the children were kept safe from "sexual risks." Outcomes were positive for a higher proportion of the 19 in foster care than the 21 in residential care, but the authors warn that the young people in residential care were older and more likely to be behaviorally disturbed at the start of the placement. The residential units were extremely varied, including children's homes, secure accommodation, and specialist group care. Thirty-two percent of those in foster care and 19% of those in residential care were rated as having good outcomes, 47% and 38% fair, and 21% and 43% poor. Thirty-six percent of the "sexually abusing" but only 11% of the "sexually abused" were rated as having good outcomes. This is a complex study that should be read with care due to the differences between the groups of children, which cannot be controlled for due to the small numbers. The wealth of detail on the children's backgrounds and care histories and on the placement and helping processes adds substantially to the small amount of information on this increasingly numerous group of children in the British care system.

Turning to the recent studies focusing specifically on residential care, Sinclair and Gibbs (1998) undertook structured interviews with 223 residents of 48 children's homes and obtained data from social workers, parents, and child care staff. Twenty percent of the placements were intended to be longer stay, and the others had a range of short-term goals, including 18% with a goal of preparation for independence, and 16% a goal of preparation for long-term placement with a foster or adoptive family. Six months after the first interviews, the researchers rated the social environment of the home, an "individual misery" score, and the social worker's adjustment score based loosely on the *Looking after Children* dimensions (see later section). They concluded that homes were more likely to do well if they were small; if roles were clear and mutually compatible; if the head of home had adequate autonomy; and if the staff agreed on how the home should be run. Changes in the adjustment of the young people were small, but were more likely to be positive if the head of home had a clear philosophy about how change could be achieved and the turnover of staff and residents was not high.

Numbers in long-term group care are limited and therefore outcome studies are few and involve small numbers. Most are in-house evaluations by specialist independent sector therapeutic units. The two studies which are closest to those described in the section on U.S. provision are those of Little and Kelly (1995) and Bullock, Little, and Millham (1998). The first provides an insight into the life and thought processes of a young woman who kept a diary while in residence at the Caldecott Community, a long stay therapeutic facility. This is set in the context of a study of the outcomes for 60 children who left the community between 1986 and 1990. Outcomes were best for the subgroup of children who entered the unit from fractured families, stayed beyond school-leaving age, and managed to re-create positive links with their families. Those who had been sexually abused before joining the community and those whose entry was precipitated by behavior difficulties and who tended to be older on admission did less well. The researchers emphasize the importance of stability and emotional warmth; the significance of the period between the fifteenth and sixteenth birthday; and the willingness of the staff to welcome back on visits and continue to provide emotional and practical support for former residents.

The study by Bullock, Little, and Millham (1998) followed the progress of 204 seriously disturbed young people who had been admitted to two long-term secure treatment facilities (one run on behavioral lines and one based on psychotherapeutic treatment methods). However, the researchers found more similarities than might be expected as these different theories were adapted to the special needs of disturbed and disturbing young people living for long periods in secure conditions. "Family work, clear and realistic expectations about reasonable behavior and discipline, high stan-dards and warm relationships between staff and residents" were in evidence (p. 55), with a quarter maintaining enduring relations with staff after leaving. "Improvements in young people's functioning can be attributed to the work of the specialist centers. But it is folly to assume that behavior modification or psychotherapeutic work is in itself a solution" (p. 55).

Outcomes in the above study were related to the early histories of the young people and reasons why secure facilities were considered necessary. Outcome took into account the predicted trajectory, given what was known about earlier history, and for the secure treatment center leavers, compared favorably with those from prisons or from other local authority facilities for similarly high-risk young people. Outcomes were very poor for around 10% and better than expected for another 10%, with 80% being moderately successful or successful in some respects but not in others. Results in respect to education and employment were particularly poor, with only 8 of the 204 leavers finding skilled work. However, the "physical and psychological health of the graduates is reasonable, given the poor expectations on entry to treatment" (p. 111). Reconviction rates were lower than expected and lower than for those in the comparison groups. The nature of the treatment regime was found to be an important determinant of outcome, in the sense that treatment regimes needed to adapt to the changing needs and "life route" of the young people.

From Australia

The common professional belief in Australia is that substitute care or out-of-home care can always be provided in nonresidential settings. This runs against the U.S. experience, where it is estimated that residential programs continue to provide 17% of all out-of-home care placements (Child Welfare League of America, 1995). It also runs against recent trends in the U.K. where, after a period of decline in the use of residential care, there are attempts to make residential placements a viable alternative to foster care (Brindle, 1998).

The view that out-of-home care can always be provided in nonresidential settings has recently been questioned (Ainsworth, 1998). This questioning reflects a growing professional concern that a small but very visible group of seriously at risk youths are unable to benefit from the services that are available. This concern is voiced by most state and territory child welfare authorities who are struggling to provide appropriate care and treatment services for this group. Ainsworth (1998) argues that nonresidential services lack power and intensity and are not of adequate duration to provide for the reeducation, resocialization, or treatment need of this group. He proposes that a new generation of well-managed, non-abusive residential programs is required to meet the need of these seriously disadvantaged young people.

The decline in the use of residential placement as a form of out-of-home care has been examined by Bath (1997), who shows that in the three-year period between 1993 and 1996, the last year for which figures are available, there was a continued decrease in the use of this type of placement. In Australia generally, this decline was from 2,415 in 1993 to 1,818 in 1996, or a reduction of nearly 25%. Yet in the same time period, the number of children in out-of-home care in Australia generally rose from 12,275 in 1993 to 14,677 in 1996. These figures represent a rate of 2.7/1000 of children in the population for 1993, and 3.1/1000 for 1996. These figures indicate that Australia has a lower rate of children in out-of-home care that most comparable western countries.

The recent publication of a study by Halliday and Darmody (1999) of families that received services from Boys' Town, a residential school in New South Wales, is also informative in relation to the issue of residential care. This qualitative study tells the story of 21 parents and their desperation to find a program that could help them and their son(s) through a difficult adolescence. It outlines how vital this residential care and education program proved to be for them and how productive residential education was for their sons.

Adoption

From the U.S.

Barth (1994a, p. 625) has noted that adoption research in the U.S. "has lost its vigor and rigor in recent years." Yet, there is extensive research on the process of adoption, as seen in an annotated guide to research conducted and/or published between 1986 and 1997 (Martin, 1998). However, summarizing this research presents quite a challenge, especially because of measurement issues in many studies in respect to such aspects as lack of specificity regarding age, diverse circumstances at placement, and variations in demographic and other characteristics. Moreover, much adoption research is about adoption of infants or very young children and there has been little examination of the long-term effects of childhood adoption in adulthood (Smyer et al., 1998).

Various studies have focused on indicators of success in adoptive placement in general, including placement stability, protection from re-abuse, achievement of developmental outcomes, and child satisfaction. The evidence suggests that, in respect to these indicators, adoptions have advantages over other permanency planning options such as long-term family foster care for younger children, and appear worth the calculated risk that they might disrupt (Barth & Berry, 1994). However, children between 12 and 17 years have disruption rates ranging as high as 47%, versus 15% for adoptions involving children between six and eight, and 7% of adoptions of children up to age five (Barth & Berry, 1994, pp. 337–338).

In line with the above, in a review of studies on the outcome of older child and adolescent adoption, Haugaard, Wojslawowicz, and Palmer (1999, p. 61) reported that "the research demonstrates that children adopted at older ages are more likely to exhibit higher levels of some problem behaviors than children adopted at younger ages." For example, in a longitudinal investigation involving 4,682 adopted young people, Sharma, McGue, and Benson (1996a and 1996b) concluded that those adopted after 10 years of age were more likely than those adopted at a younger age to engage in licit and illicit drug use and antisocial behavior. However, the children adopted past age 10 turned out to be no different from those adopted at a younger age on measures of negativity, emotionality, prosocial behavior, optimism, and school adjustment.

On the basis of the above review, Haugaard, Wojslawowicz, and Palmer (1999, p. 69) offer a number of important possibilities for further investigations:

- The problem behaviors that are more likely to occur in older-child or adolescent adoptions than in adoptions of younger children are antisocial, delinquent, and hostile behaviors.

- There are few differences in internalizing problems (e.g., depression, anxiety) between children adopted at younger and older ages.

- The adoptions of older girls may be more likely to disrupt than the adoptions of older boys, even though the boys appear to engage in more problem behaviors than the girls.

- The placement of sibling groups together may have a more positive influence on success of older-child adoptions than on younger-child adoptions.

- The adoptions of many older children and adolescents are successful, even though they may be stressful to the families and to the adoptees.

Smyer et al. (1998) emphasize that a life-span perspective is essential in assessing the impact of stressful life events on adopted children. In their intensive study of Swedish twins who had been adopted as children, these researchers point to the complexity of adoption and its impact and conclude:

> In particular, the results reflect the important mediating role of childhood socioeconomic status, suggesting that the stress of adoption itself is mediated by the type of rearing environment provided by the adoption process. (Smyer et al., 1998, p. 191)

The child welfare literature also reflects substantial efforts by agencies, researchers, and practitioners to expand knowledge about the familial and systemic factors that contribute to successful adoption for sibling groups, children with disabilities, adolescents, and children placed transracially. Much of this research concerns the process rather than the outcome of adoptions. In particular, various authors have examined the multiple challenges involved in adoption of children with "special needs," including "older children, children of color, children with physical, mental, or emotional problems, and children who are part of a sibling group" (McKenzie, 1993, p. 62). The experiences of these children often involve barriers to adoption, such as the following:

- Parenting some children can be very challenging;

- Preparation for adoption is complex, as many children are initially resistant to being adopted;

- Developing a relationship with the adoptive family may be a struggle for some children, particularly those with attachment problems;

- Difficulty of some children, who are developmentally delayed or mentally retarded and lack cognitive skills, to understand and integrate the abstract concepts related to adoption. (Rykus & Hughes, 1998, pp. 886-887)

Research, however, has shown that "on balance, adoption outcomes for children with special needs are distinctly positive" (Rosenthal, 1993, p. 77). The success of such placements can be enhanced through sophisticated child advocacy and adoption advocacy (Andersen, 1997); intensive adoption recruitment efforts (Lakin & Whitfield, 1997); and further attention to the service needs of children and families, through provision of accurate background information, adoption subsidies, postadoption services, and other resources and supports for the adoptive family (Groze, 1996; Rosenthal, 1993, pp. 84-85). In her study of outcomes of special needs adoptions, McRoy (1999 pp. 241-252), offers a series of practice recommendations, including:

- Accurate and complete documentation of all case activities;

- Use of "Court Appointed Special Advocates";

- Increased recruitment and training of prospective adoptive families;

- Improved family assessments for foster and adoptive families; and

- Addressing issues of loss with children and birth and adoptive parents.

Additionally, it is urgent to focus on reform of services for children of color by targeting such areas as racism and cultural insensitivity and instituting stronger advocacy efforts. In this connection, a demonstration project conducted between 1995 and 1998 throughout the U.S. by the W. K. Kellogg's Families for Kids Initiative identified the following principles of reform:

- Empowering the community, especially families and community representatives.

- Reordering funding patterns toward better utilization for services to families.

- Revising service delivery systems so that they may be more culturally appropriate, collaborative, simple, effective and accessible.

- Strengthening advocacy for families and children of color, through strong and centralized organizations (W. K. Kellogg Foundation, undated).

Sibling Groups. There has been limited research in regard to sibling groups, as the pattern in practice has been to place siblings either separately in foster or adoptive homes, or together with foster families (Smith, 1996), with adverse consequences for their development (Kosonen, 1997). Often, placement decisions are guided not by the value of keeping siblings together, but by pragmatic reasons "such as problems in recruiting suitable foster homes, . . . children's gender or ethnicity, . . . children's age, sibling group size," and related factors (Smith, 1996, p. 360). Also, state or voluntary agencies lack the up-front money to place siblings together in foster care. Once separated in foster care, children are much less likely to be placed together in an adoptive placement. In addition, workers may be unaware that foster children have siblings (though statistics suggest that 65 to 85% of children who enter foster care have at least one sibling). (Riggs, 1999, p. 2).

Available studies indicate that the adoption of sibling groups requires extensive support and commitment on the part of public and private agencies. It also calls for adoptive parents with the ability to organize, set priorities, and delegate (Ward, 1987); close agency supervision and availability of adoptive parent support groups (Depp, 1983); and intensive family preservation services (Pecora et al., 2000). Also, in a study of successful adoptive families, Groze (1996, p. 77) found some "support for the expectation that siblings placed together would have better outcomes than siblings separated." This study reinforces practitioner wisdom regarding the need to provide extensive and ongoing supports to sibling groups and their adoptive families.

Children with Physical and/or Mental Disabilities. There is evidence that children entering out-of-home care "typically have significant physical, mental health, and developmental problems" (Simms et al., 1999, p. 166; Landsverk & Garland, 2000). For example, adopted children are disproportionately represented in child psychiatric populations, in part as a result of genetic and environmental factors contributing to the development of psychological disorders. However, we should avoid "the simplistic assumption that psychological problems in adopted children and adolescents are primarily attributed to the fact of adoption, per se" (Ingersoll, 1997, p. 66). Instead, it is essential "to explore *all* factors which might bear on the child's adjustment, including past and current patterns of dysfunction within the parents and other family members" (Ingersoll, 1997, p. 67).

Indeed, various projects indicate that the adoption of children with physical or mental problems can be successfully accomplished through multiple supports and approaches. These include special education programs (Brodzinsky & Steiger, 1991; Groze, 1996); counseling, physical therapy and respite care (Lightburn & Pine, 1996); financial assistance to adoptive families; and provision of postadoption services (McKenzie, 1993; Rosenthal & Groze, 1994; Smith & Howard, 1999). Such supports are essential in promoting successful adaptation and development (Gross & Sussman, 1997). Although most adoptees, according to the professional literature, are within the normal range of functioning, as a group they tend to be more vulnerable to emotional, behavioral, and academic problems than their peers living with their birth families (Brodzinsky, 1993). However, as shown in research on adoption of developmentally vulnerable black children, for example, through professional and family support, children function relatively well and have positive self-esteem (Hoopes et al., 1997).

Adolescents. Teenagers present a special challenge in adoption, in part since adolescence is a time of renewed and intense conflict, heightened concerns about identity, and strivings toward independence. However, the research evidence also indicates that adolescents can be successfully adopted, as long as extensive services and supports are available to them and their birth as well as adoptive families. This is particularly important, as older adopted children experience a range of unresolved feelings along with their normative adolescent struggles (Robinson, 1998).

Especially crucial in the successful adoption of adolescents are intensive services and supports during the immediate postplacement readjustment process (Pinderhughes, 1996); "wraparound" service strategies that include a range of individually tailored services (Clark et al., 1996); intensive family preservation services particularly in placements threatened by disruptions (Pecora et al., 2000); and a continuum of care for adolescents placed in residential treatment facilities before or after adoption (Young et al., 1992). Also relevant is the work of Smith and Howard (1999) in the area of postadoption services. On the basis of their four-year study of the Adoption Preservation Program in Illinois, these authors offer a range of recommendations for services to adoptive families and children during the postadoption period. These include:

- thorough preparation of adoptive families;

- making preventive services available;

- closing the case based on family need rather than imposed time limits;

- continuing development of respite care; and

- ending adoption with support for all parties when this is in the child's best interests.

As an alternative to adoption, in the U.S. subsidized guardianship is being tested through demonstrations in various states, although evaluative results are not as yet available. The largest of these projects is in Illinois and involves 2,000 caregivers and 1,000 children age 11 years or over (Testa, 1999). A similar demonstration based in Maryland involves a five-year testing of the impact of a $300 per month guardianship cash subsidy on the well-being of children and caregivers (Orlin, 1999). Initial reports indicate that subsidized guardianship is enabling permanency to be established for a number of children. Noticeably, these are older children where parental rights have been terminated and who sometimes age out of the child welfare system before adoptive parents can be found.

Although, as seen in this section, there has been some useful research regarding adoption of older children, further outcome studies addressing the following questions would be useful:

- Are there characteristics of the older children or of their behaviors at the time of placement that predict the types or intensity of the problems that they are likely to exhibit?

- Are there characteristics of adoptive families that are associated with the ability to provide stable adoptive homes to older children and adolescents?

- Is adoption the best placement option for older children or adolescents, or are other types of placements more likely to be successful?

- Are there characteristics of the older child or adolescent that predict whether an adoptive placement or another type of placement would be most stable and beneficial to the child? (Haugaard et al., 1999, p. 69).

Transracial Adoption. As for transracial adoption, the literature reflects considerable controversy (Haugaard et al., 1997). On the one hand, there has been major opposition to the practice of transracial adoption of black children, through leadership of the National Association of Black Social Workers (NABSW); since 1972, the Association has continued to call on public and private child welfare agencies to "cease and desist" transracial placements, which are considered "a growing threat to the preservation of the black family" (Downs et al., 1996, p. 355). In addition, the NABSW is greatly concerned that transracial adoption of black children threatens their growth and development and the sense of pride and self-identification that is essential for normal development. Along the same lines, Hollingsworth (1998) argues for promoting same-race adoption of children of color through such means as policies favoring adoption by foster parents, aggressive recruitment of families of color, and research on the impact of transracial placement on children's functioning and development. Goddard, L.L., 1996) notes that the research evidence regarding the impact of transracial adoption is imprecise, especially since there has been limited examination of subtle effects, such as individualism, cultural denigration, racial separation, and self-hate. As a result, he advocates further use of a Black developmental perspective and understanding of the influences of culture in adoption (Goddard, L.L., 1996).

On the other hand, other researchers report that most minority children placed in transracial adoption adjust successfully, as reflected in a number of studies. Vroegh (1997) indicates that black adolescents adopted into white families were found to have good or very good self-esteem and to be well adjusted. Simon et al. (1994) argue for transracial adoption on the basis of a 20-year study of transracial adoptees and their families that demonstrates the children's positive adjustment. Silverman (1993) notes that most transracial adoptees have a sense of identity with their racial heritage, due to the support of the adoptive parents. Bush (1995) delineates factors that promote racial identity and self-esteem in adoptees; these include living in a multiethnic community, having adoptive parents who accept the child's cultural heritage, and regular exposure to persons who share the child's ethnic background.

In considering the practice of transracial adoption and its impact on children, it is useful to "heed the caveats enunciated by black professionals about potential dangers that lurk down the developmental road" (Smith, 1997, p. 105), as well as increase opportunities for black families to adopt. It should also be emphasized that "agencies specializing in achieving same-race adoptive placement have been extremely successful in achieving same-race adoptive placement for African-American children; [yet] funding and support for some of these initiatives have been withheld due to federal and state legislation designed to limit the consideration of race as a major factor in the selection of adoptive families" (McRoy et al., 1997, p. 85). At the same time, "the practice of transracial adoption should be considered as an option *as long as* the research shows that children of transracial families thrive in it" (Smith, 1997, p. 105).

Open Versus Closed Adoption. Finally, it should be noted that in the U.S. there is a growing controversy over the matter of open versus closed adoption, particularly in relation to older children. Although much has been written about this issue in the professional literature, there is little research available. While some authors argue that open adoption interferes with the process of bonding between the child and adoptive parents (Kraft et al., 1985), other investigators have found that older children need and can benefit from continuing relationships with their birth parents.

In a recent study on the outcome of adoptions in which some form of contact had been maintained with the birth family, Grotevant and McRoy (1998) concluded that this is a complex and subtle matter. For instance, parents in fully disclosed adoptions talked about adoption more openly with their children; birth mothers were able to grieve the child's loss; and relationships between birth mothers and adoptive parents and children evolved appropriately. On the other hand, there were no significant differences between open and closed adoptions in relation to the adopters' level of satisfaction, children's self-esteem, and children's social-emotional adjustment. While further research in this area is essential, there is evidence that open adoption can appropriately be viewed as an *enrichment* to a stable placement, not a *palliative* of a troubled one (Pecora et al., 2000).

From the U.K.

The most comprehensive sources of information on numbers and types of children being adopted in the U.K. are the Department of Health and the Welsh, Scottish and Northern Ireland Office Annual Statistics on children looked after by local authorities and Health Trusts. The 1997 volume for England notes that roughly a third of all children adopted during the year had been looked after by local authorities prior to adoption and that most of the remaining two-thirds have been adopted by stepparents or relatives. The total number of children who ceased to be looked after because they were adopted fell from 2,500 in 1992/93 to an estimated 1,900 in 1996/97. The British Agencies for Adoption and Fostering (BAAF) (Ivaldi, 1998) provide a commentary on these statistics. In 1996/97 more than half of these children were under five years of age at the time of adoption.

Earlier adoption outcome studies in the U.K. suffer in their usefulness from a lack of specificity about the age and circumstances of the children at the time of placement, a deficit which more recent studies have attempted to correct. The following overview will concentrate on British children adopted by parents to whom they were not related, and will consider separately children placed as infants and older-child placements.

Children Adopted as Infants. Those long-term outcome studies that have followed infant adoptees into adulthood by definition describe practice and populations of children placed 20 or more years ago. More recent studies can only provide interim outcome data but give valuable descriptive information about children's and adoptive family experiences and about practice.

The two most important early outcome studies of infant adoptions are those of McWhinnie (1967) and Raynor (1980). Raynor reports on a follow-up study of young adults who were placed for adoption as infants, some directly placed with the adoptive families and some placed initially in foster care "with a view to adoption." Although there were the usual problems with tracing a full cohort, it seems likely that the breakdown rate was somewhere between 5% and 10%. When interviewed, 80% of the adoptees expressed satisfaction with their upbringing, and 85% of the adopters were satisfied with their experience of adoption.

McWhinnie's (1967) retrospective study involved detailed interviews with 52 adult adoptees and in some cases interviews with family doctors. A range of outcome indicators was used, on the basis of which it was concluded that 21 had a very good or good outcome, but 21 had experienced and were still experiencing difficulties that were in some way related to their adoption. Information was not available in ten cases. More recently, Lambert and Streather (1980) and Maughan and Pickles (1990) attempted to locate and follow up 182 children adopted before the age of 7 (75% placed before 12 weeks of age), drawn from a cohort of 17,000 children born in 1958. They compared their development with that of children born out of wedlock but not adopted and of a random subsample of children who were brought up by both birth parents. They note the importance of controlling for a range of variables, since the adoptees were generally brought up in more favorable economic and social circumstances than either of the other two groups. Of the 182 studied at the age of 7, 115 were traced and assessed at age 11, but only 82 were available for interview at the age of 16. This loss to the sample (which was even higher for those born out of wedlock but not adopted) has to be born in mind when considering the findings. At the age of 7, the adoptees were doing better than those who remained with their single parent and as well or better on most measures than those who had been born to married couples. At the age of 11, however, "especially when their more favored social situation had been taken into account, their adjustment appeared to have deteriorated and was closer to that of the illegitimate than the legitimate group" (Maughan & Pickles, 1990, p. 43). This broad pattern was also found when the young people reached the age of 16. The researchers noted in particular that the adoptees had higher rates of anxiety and peer relationship problems than those who had lived with both birth parents. By the age of 23, the adopted women were similar to the "born legitimate" group, but there was a trend (which did not reach statistical significance) for the young men who had been adopted to have difficulties in settling in employment, and more of them had experienced the breakdown of a partner relationship.

The above studies report on placements made when prevailing views on out of wedlock birth and adoptions as well as adoption practice were very different. Howe's (1996) study reports on a series of interviews with 120 adopters of over 300 children who are now young adults, most of whom were placed as infants. Because of the nonrandom nature of the sample, the research cannot provide data on success and breakdown rates. However, the detailed interview data are rich sources of information about patterns of development as seen through the eyes of the adopters, and about adopter satisfaction. The four broad patterns identified were: secure children, anxious to please children, angry children, and uninvolved and wary children. Howe relates these patterns to the nature of the child's early attachments and experiences of parenting.

Thoburn (1991) and Sellick and Thoburn (1996) reviewed the findings of a range of British and overseas infant adoption outcome studies. They concluded that somewhere between 5% and 10% of children placed as infants will experience placement disruption, and that around 80% of the adopters and of the adult adoptees will express general satisfaction with the growing-up experience. However, when problems do arise, they appear to be associated with issues of identity, and this is more common with children of minority ethnic origin who are placed transracially. An unknown proportion of these adult adoptees placed as infants who expressed general satisfaction with the experience of adoption are also "troubled" by identity issues. Many of these adult adoptees do not seek to resolve these difficulties by looking for further information about their birth parents until the adoptive parents have died or some particular event in their adult life such as childbirth or illness causes them to take steps to seek out further information or actual contact with birth parents.

Useful sources of data come from the annual reports of postadoption centers or adoption agencies. The Children's Society (Howe & Feast, 2000) and Barnardos (Pugh & Schofield, 1999) are particularly rich sources of information. A further useful source is the work of Triseliotis, Shireman, and Hundleby (1997), which combines British research with material from the U.S. and Scandinavia. A later prospective study on infant adoption (Rutter and the ERA Study Team, 1998) compares the placement of children from Romania with infants adopted within the U.K. and follows them until they are aged seven years. Marked differences are found between the two groups, which are associated with early privation and deprivation for the Romanian children. The researchers report that the Romanian adoptees, in the main, catch up on physical and cognitive development, but concerns persist in the area of prosocial development, especially for those placed when over the age of two.

Neil (in press) surveyed children recently placed for adoption by adoption agencies when under the age of four. She found that only 14% were relinquished at birth; 24% were relinquished in more complex circumstances, often after living for a period with birth parents and having experienced neglect, maltreatment, or rejection. The remaining 62% were placed for adoption from care against the wishes of their parents, often following episodes of maltreatment and multiple placement. This is a longitudinal study, which focuses particularly on postplacement contact with birth relatives, but no outcome data are yet available. Neil (1999) reports on the placement and contact arrangements for the sibling groups within this study.

Children Placed When Past Infancy. Department of Health statistics (Department of Health, 1999) show that the proportion of those aged five or over who left care and were adopted has fallen gradually since its peak in 1992/93, but started to rise again in 1998/ 99. In 1996/97, 44% had been looked after for two years or more before they were adopted and these are more likely to be the older children. It is not known what proportion of those adopted by foster carers were initially placed as short-term foster children and subsequently adopted by that family, and what proportion were adopted by foster carers with whom they had been placed with the intention that it would be a permanent placement. Thus, in respect of older children, it is difficult to disentangle long-term foster placements and placement for adoption of children looked after by local authorities.

The adoption of older children, many of whom have physical or learning difficulties or behavioral problems due to early adverse living circumstances, separation, loss, and maltreatment, has been well researched in the U.K. Sellick and Thoburn (1996) and Triseliotis et al. (1997) review the main body of research and the Department of Health (1999) provides an overview of the most recent studies. Thoburn (1991), as part of a review of permanent family placement policy in the U.K. in the 1980s (Fratter et al., 1991) reports on a survey of 1,165 children placed with permanent foster families or adopters between 1980 and 1985. Thoburn et al. (2000) report on a long-term study of 297 of these children who were of minority ethnic origin and give a detailed account of 51 of the young people when they were aged between 10 and 30. In this and the 1991 study, logit analysis is used to identify characteristics of the children and placements that were independently associated with placement lasting or breakdown rates.

The conclusion from the above British studies is that around one in five placements of older children or those with special needs will break down before the child reaches independence. Breakdown rates increase with age at placement, with around half of the children aged between ten and twelve likely to experience the breakdown of their adoptive or permanent foster care placement. All researchers come to similar conclusions about the factors that increase the risk of breakdown for children of all ages. Having been abused or mal-treated is associated with greater risk even for the youngest children (Gibbons et al., 1995; Thoburn, 1991), as is having behavioral or emotional problems or being described as "institutionalized" at the time of placement. If variables such as age at placement are held constant, breakdown rates for white children or those with two parents of the same minority ethnic origin are not statistically different, though some researchers report a higher breakdown rate for children of mixed race parentage (Thoburn, 1991).

Thoburn et al. (2000) found that there was no overall difference in breakdown rates between children placed in ethnically matched placements and those placed transracially. However, in light of other data from this study, they conclude that families of an ethnic origin other than that of the child have additional difficulties in helping young people confront racism and develop positive racial and cultural identity. They therefore conclude that the guidance in the England and Wales Children Act 1989 that children should, wher-ever possible, be placed in an ethnically matched foster and adoptive families is appropriate. However, if transracial placement is neces-sary, (as, for example, when children have become securely attached to foster parents of a different ethnic origin and a further move is likely to cause harm), the evidence is that some white families can successfully parent children of minority ethnic origin and help them realize a positive sense of themselves as adopted people of a minor-ity culture.

Factors associated with greater stability of placement include the child having a physical disability or a learning difficulty and being placed as part of a sibling group in the same family. Children who have contact with birth parents in some studies are found to have a greater chance of successful placement, and in other studies birth parent contact is a neutral factor. Thoburn's (1991) cohort of 1,165 adoptive or permanent foster family placements was large enough to allow logit analysis; it concluded that face to face contact after placement was associated with a lower rate of placement breakdown (estimated coefficient 0.708; p<.01). In this study, when other variables were held constant, there was no difference in breakdown rates between those placed for adoption and those placed for permanent foster care. However, Triseliotis and Russell (1984) and Hill et al. (1989) found that adopted children who had previously experienced foster care said that they were glad that they had been adopted. They also reported that the adopted children had higher educational achievements than those who were fostered.

Research has led to few statistically significant associations between characteristics of the adoptive or foster family and those of the child, although several studies conclude that, in cases of children placed where the new parents have a child of their own of the same age or a younger age than the foster child, there is a greater likelihood of placement breakdown. Turning to the other measures of success, although earlier problems may be alleviated, adoption cannot be seen as a "cure" for children who were behaviorally or emotionally disturbed at the time of placement. There does appear to be some evidence that young people placed in stable adoption or permanent foster care make substantial progress in their late teens and early twenties, and that their relationships with adoptive or foster families which have been shaky improve as the young person moves through the early adult years (Howe, 1997; Thoburn et al., 1999).

From Australia

Once again, there is a paucity of Australian research in the area of adoption. Some research reports may have been completed by state and territory child welfare authorities. Unfortunately, where they do exist, these reports generally have limited circulation.

The low number of children who are being adopted in Australia (668 in 1995–1996) may account for the almost total absence of research on this topic. A recent Aust-rom keyword search of the Institute of Family Studies database identified only one recent research study. This study was of the well-being of 4- to 16-year-old intercountry adoptees, entitled "Intercountry Adoption families in Western Australia . . ." (1996). The focus of this study may reflect the fact that 56% of children adopted (274 in Australia out of a total of 668 in 1995–1996) were born overseas.

The continuing support for overseas adoption is also contro-versial (Forell, 1991). However, in 1997, the Australian government re-signed the Hague Convention on Intercountry Adoption (Hague Convention, 1997). This is surprising, given the monu-mental Australian evidence of the negative effect of child migra-tion (Humphreys, 1995) and the consequence of the separation of Aboriginal children from their families and culture of origin (Human Rights and Equal Opportunities Commission, 1997). Parallels between these practices and overseas adoption are acute, since both may separate children from extended family and sources of racial, religious, and cultural identity.

Notes

1. The address of the New South Wales Association of Children's Welfare Agencies is 323 Castlereagh Street, Sydney, NSW 2000, Australia.

2. For a comprehensive discussion of foster care theory and practice that reflects recent research, see Martin (2000).

3. Gilligan (2000) calls attention to the sparse literature on the roles and experiences of men as foster carers, which is true in Australia and the U.S. as well. He also reports on a small exploratory study of foster fathers, showing that they play an important role in supporting their partners as the primary carers and in involving foster youths in activities outside the home.

4. See Stein (1995) for extensive description of current residen-tial treatment programs for children and youths, as well as issues, principles, and techniques. Also see Alwon et al. (2000) for presen-tation of strategic intervention approaches to support family-cen-tered practice in residential settings, and Bass et al. (2000) for assessment of a family-centered, strengths-based model of practice in children's residential settings.

Chapter 3

Outcome Research on Recent Service Initiatives

In this chapter, we review outcome research on newer service initiatives, including family preservation, family reunification, "Looking After Children," family group decision-making, shared family care, "wraparound" services, and preparation for independent living services (also known as leaving care or after care services). Family reunification services are included since, as a formal program, they are relatively new in most agency settings. There is an overlap between family reunification studies and studies of independent living services. The former are mainly concerned with younger children and the latter with older adolescents who have become separated from birth relatives and move into independent living on leaving care. However, some reunification studies give information about teenagers who go back to their extended families or home communities, and some independent living studies describe young people who return to their birth relatives.

Family Preservation Services

From the U.S.

In the U.S. family preservation covers an array of programs with diverse philosophies, types and intensity of services, and target groups. Services range from highly specialized, time-limited and intensive programs to generic family support programs.[1] But the outcome research does not always identify the specific nature of the services provided. In his analysis of a range of studies involving primarily intensive services, Pecora (1994) reports mixed findings in regard to placement prevention rates, ranging from 0% to 40% (Feldman, 1991; Pecora, 1991; Wells & Biegel, 1991). Moreover, in most studies there were no significant differences between the treatment and control groups in relation to placement prevention. A major issue in this regard is that intensive family preservation services (IFPS) have been aimed at families with at least one child at risk of "imminent placement" (Walton & Denby, 1997). However, it has been difficult in most programs as well as research studies to identify and target children who were truly at risk of out-of-home placement—that is, children who would clearly have been placed if IFPS had not been provided. In fact "most families who get referred to family preservation programs are cases in which there is not much likelihood of placement even without the services" (Rzepnicki, 1994, p. 304). As a result, the findings of outcome studies are inconclusive. Partly for this reasons, more recently researchers have been emphasizing that outcome criteria beyond placement prevention should be incorporated into evaluation studies, including in particular improvement in child, parent, and family functioning (Pecora, 1994; Rzepnicki, 1994).

In a related study, Meezan and McCroskey (1996) and McCroskey and Meezan (1997) examined the outcomes of family preservation services for abusive and neglectful families in Los Angeles, the largest county in the U.S., with 6.6 million adults and 2.6 million children. The population in Los Angeles is increasingly diverse, especially among its children under 18 years: in 1990, 50% of the children were Latino (primarily Mexican-American), 27% were white, 12% were black, and 10% were Asian American. The study, conducted between 1989 and 1994, focused on changes in family functioning during the three-month service period and one year after case closing.

The key questions were (Meezan & McCroskey, 1996, pp. 10-11):

1. Is there a change in the functioning of abusive/neglectful families over time, and can such changes be attributed to the programs of the two agencies under study?

2. What factors are associated with positive outcomes for families and children participating in the experimental programs?

3. Do ratings of family functioning differ when information is collected by practitioners rather than research interviewers?

4. To what extent is participation in the experimental programs associated with decreased need for other child welfare services, including out-of-home placement?

Families were referred to the above project by the county public
welfare agency, on the basis of the caseworkers' judgment of the
need for services rather than the more typical criterion of "imminent
risk." A total of 240 families were randomly assigned to either a
group receiving *intensive family preservation services* from two private, nonprofit agencies or a comparison group receiving *regular
public agency services*. The latter consisted of limited contacts between
caseworkers and family members. The study employed a modified
experimental design with a one-year follow-up. Meezan and
McCroskey (1996) collected data primarily by means of an ecologi-
cally-oriented and practice-based Family Assessment Form cover-
ing most areas of child and family functioning. In addition, they used
standardized instruments, including an inventory of parent mental
health, the Achenbach Child Behavior Check List (for children age 6
or over), the Home Observation for Measurement of the Environment (for children under age 6), and a caregiver satisfaction survey.
Caseworkers and families reported small but significant improvements in family functioning for the experimental group families, but
not for the comparison group families. The improvements occurred
during the year after completion of the service, specifically in the
areas of *living conditions* and *financial interactions*. Parents noted
more concrete improvements such as housing.

As the authors point out (Meezan & McCroskey, 1996, p. 15), this
design has various drawbacks:

1. The absolute effectiveness of the service cannot be ascer-
tained because they are not compared with a "no service"
condition.

2. The impact of the treatment is underestimated, since comparisons are to a "regularly" served rather than an unserved
group.

3. The research questions are focused on comparative rather
than absolute effectiveness.

A related study by Schuerman, Rzepnicki, and Littell (1994) was even more extensive than the Los Angeles study, as it involved a statewide and multifaceted evaluation of the Families First initiative, a placement prevention program focusing on families officially reported for child abuse and neglect throughout the state of Illinois. The program was administered by the state, with services provided on a contractual basis by 60 private agencies to 6,522 families.

The design involved: (1) collection of descriptive data on all Families First cases and programs; (2) an experiment testing program effectiveness, with 995 families randomly assigned to a Families First group receiving intensive services and 569 families assigned to a control group receiving regular agency services; and (3) a longitudinal survey of parents in a representative sample of cases and programs, to assess the impact on child and family functioning. The findings indicate that family preservation services did not produce a significant effect on the risk of placement, subsequent maltreatment, child and family functioning, or case closure. In short, although the authors conclude that their message "is one of caution but not despair" (p. 229), the Families First program's did not achieve the objective of prevention of placement in out-of-home care.

The above study can be criticized on methodological grounds. For example, the experimental variable (the nature of services) was inadequately defined and operationalized: within broad parameters, each agency was allowed to define what constituted family preservation services. Moreover, while the experiment was rigorously conducted, "the large and interrelated differences among sites, programs and families create problems in assessing service effectiveness for sub populations, to such an extent that it is unclear what was being tested" (Nelson, 1996, p. 118). Nelson (1996) also questions the extent to which "family preservation" was actually being evaluated and points to the way in which hallmarks of family preservation services, such as time-limited service and the mutual setting of goals by workers and families, were not observed (Nelson, 1996). On the other hand, Maluccio (1995), when reviewing the same study, draws attention to the complexity of the phenomena under scrutiny and the limitations of the research methodology. Despite the methodological limitations evident in this study, Schuerman, Rzepnicki, and Littell (1994) contribute to the discourse on family preservation services by stimulating further debate regarding their nature, role, and effectiveness. In particular, administrators, policy-makers and researchers are challenged to reexamine their assumptions, clarify their ideas and expectations, and redirect their research and program development efforts toward more realistic goals.

In recent years there have also been various investigations of brief IFPS. Blythe, Salley, and Jayaratne (1994) examined 12 such studies, including program evaluation efforts as well as quasi-experimental and experimental designs. They found that, with some notable exceptions, the 12 studies "as a whole provide some support for the effectiveness of family preservation service" (p. 223). How-ever, they also identified a number of recurring concerns, including:

- the indication that the subjects were not at 'imminent risk' of out-of-home placement;

- the unclear nature of the intervention provided to the experimental and control groups; and

- the inability to make comparisons across diverse studies due to lack of uniformity in relation to definition of such variables as child placement, intensity and nature of services, and follow-up intervals.

On the basis of the above review, Blythe et al. (1994, p. 223) concluded as follows:

Clearly, intensive family preservation programs have the potential to help many families avoid unnecessary place-ment of children, especially when the programs reach the appropriate population. In a short period, several studies have been produced that advance the knowledge of family preservation practice and point to challenges for the next round of research. Although family preservation programs have been evaluated more frequently than other programs for this population, lingering skepticism regarding their effectiveness calls for additional and more rigourous research.

In response to such skepticism, Kelly and Blythe (2000) state that "family preservation programs must begin to collect performance data, build in quality assurance measures, and provide ongoing training based on the results of their monitoring mechanisms" (p. 38). All of this would help to ensure that these services reach their full potential with diverse population groups.

There is also a large group of programs in the U.S. known as home-based services, family-based services, or family centered services, that aim to prevent the placement of children in out-of-home care and claim to be family preservation programs. This is not unlike Australia, where programs are beginning to use this terminology even when established practice seems to remain largely unaltered. Many of these programs do not meet the intent or operational criteria mentioned above and as such should probably be excluded from this category (Bath and Haapala, 1994). As a consequence, evaluations of family preservation services have been bedevilled by a lack of agreement as to exactly what is being evaluated (Nelson, 1996; Rossi, 1991).

There is clearer evidence of outcomes when within-program rather than between-program evaluations of the outcomes of intensive family preservation services are made (Curry, 1991). Bath and Haapala (1993) reported differential outcomes in an examination of 530 families from the Homebuilders management information system database for the period 1985–1988. The families were classified into three maltreatment groups based on the reason for referral, whether because of physical abuse, neglect, or mixed physical abuse and neglect. The results indicated that the majority of the 854 children, ranging in age from 7.1 to 10.1 years, from these families avoided placement:

> Twelve months post intervention the placement rate was 13.9% which means that 86.1% of all the children remained with their family. The rates for the physical abuse, the neglect and the mixed physical abuse groups were 9.6%,

15.3% and 24.2%, respectively. However, because differences between groups in the number of at-risk children, the placement of the oldest child at-risk in each family is a more valid comparative measure. These rates are 11.5% for the physical abuse group, 20.9% for the neglect group, and 31.0% for the mixed physical abuse and neglect group, with an overall placement rate of 17.1% [X^2 (2:N = 426) = 14.4, p = .0008]." (Bath & Haapala, 1993, p. 220)

This evidence shows that this particular family preservation program is most successful with families referred because of physical abuse only. The majority of children in neglecting families and those with a history of multiple maltreatment were also able to avoid placement, but the risk of failure was considerably greater for them than that for physically abused children. Practitioners need to note these results and the age of the children (7.1 to 10.1 years) in the sample, as these results may not be valid for older children, particularly adolescents.

Certainly the evaluation of family preservation programs continues to be fraught with methodological difficulties. Reviews of the research have raised many issues (Bath & Haapala, 1994; Berry, 1997; Pecora et al., 1995; Rossi, 1991). First, there is the difficulty in developing clearly defined models of the range of family preservation programs and the component services in ways that allow for the measurement of the separate elements of the intervention. Then there is the problem of ensuring that these programs and services are only targeted at families with children that are genuinely at "imminent risk of out-of-home placement," which is vital to any evaluation of their placement prevention capacity. This continues to be a serious challenge (Berry, 1997; Pecora et al., 1995; Rossi, 1991; Walton & Denby, 1997).

There are also issues about the purpose and scope of any evaluation. Is it to "monitor program implementation, measure client outcomes, track child placement rates, determine differential effects among certain client groups, gather cost-effectiveness data, or some other purpose?" (Pecora et al., 1995, p. 11). Given this situation, Maluccio's (1995) plea for family preservation practitioners and researchers "to hang in there" but temper their enthusiasm about program effectiveness and their critique of these services seems entirely appropriate. Overall, the U.S. evaluations do not provide sufficient evidence that family preservation services are significantly more effective than more traditional forms of family casework (Lindsey, 1994).

Accordingly, those who have urged practitioners to move more slowly in the light of the limited knowledge of the impact of family preservation programs and to strike a balance between family preservation and child protection continue to deserve attention (Ainsworth, 1993; Lindsey, 1994; Wald, 1988; Maluccio et al., 1994). In addition, although we appreciate the importance and relevance of rigorous outcome evaluations for political as well as professional reasons, we need to acknowledge that child welfare programs such as family preservation must become more "mature" before we can adequately assess their effectiveness. At this point in the development of practice and knowledge in the field of child welfare, we would argue that much of effort ought to go into evaluation of *formative* or *process* evaluation more than *summative* or *outcome* evaluation. For example, specific components need to be clearly delineated, tested, and refined before these programs may be replicated and compared to one another in a systematic fashion. As Berry (1997, p. 160) indicates:

> Once a program is relatively certain of performing not only consistent but also quality operations, an evaluation of whether these operations affect clients in the theoretically expected manner is appropriate, but not before this time.[2]

From the U.K.

In the U.K. there is a long tradition of community-based services to prevent the need for out-of-home care, mainly provided by voluntary child care agencies such as Family Service Units and the Family Welfare Agency, more recently joined by the other big voluntary child care agencies including Barnardos and the National Children's Home. Legislation in 1963 required statutory agencies to provide or to commission "preventive" services. Building on this tradition, the

England and Wales Children Act 1989 and the Children Act (Scotland) 1991 require local authorities or public health care bodies to provide family support services to children defined as "in need." These services must include accommodation and respite services to children, if appropriate, together with their parents. There has been a much publicized debate (referred to as the "re-focusing debate"), about the appropriate balance between family support work and child protection investigations (Department of Health, 1997b).

The readers of this review will find a useful source of information about the Department of Health "re-focusing initiative" in an edited volume by Parton (1997). The term "family preservation services" is not used, but many of these services have some or all of the characteristics that, in the U.S., go under the broader interpretation of that label. The families targeted by these interventions include those at risk of maltreatment, as well as those at risk of needing out-of-home care. More recently, attention has been paid to the development of services to support families whose preteenage children are becoming involved in crime.

Extensive research has been commissioned by the Department of Health (Department of Health, 1995a and b) on services to children at risk of maltreatment. Several of the studies describe support work with cohorts of families referred because of concerns about child maltreatment (Farmer & Owen, 1995; Cleaver & Freeman, 1995; Thoburn et al., 1995). These studies focus particularly on the extent to which social workers, as required by the legislation, seek to work in partnership with parents and young people and attempt to relate this to outcomes. Utting (1995) summarizes the British and American research on family support, crime prevention, and parent education. Most British research focuses on Family Centres as settings for family support (Smith, 1996; Cannan, 1992). A wide range of interventions and support services is provided from a family center base, including volunteer home visiting schemes, the best known of which are Home Start and NEWPIN. Modest evaluations of these are summarized in Gibbons (1992). Evidence on child welfare outcomes is as yet sparse, but parental satisfaction is high for both of these and for similar, more localized schemes. Although these interventions have an impact on the lives of many children and families, and rates of satisfaction are high, systematic outcome studies are few, and generally of very small experimental projects.

Gibbons (1990) evaluated family centers and other voluntary agency initiatives in two local authorities and concluded that those local authorities that supported the growth of voluntary agencies and also allocated a social worker at an earlier stage were more likely to provide evidence of improved parental well-being over a twelve-month period. Packman and Hall (1998) show that well-planned and short-term accommodation can be a crucially important part of a family support service, a conclusion with which Aldgate and Bradley (1999) agree, drawing on their study of respite care for children whose parents are under stress. (See earlier section on foster care.)

In a study of family intervention services provided by local authorities, Pithouse and Tasiran (2000) suggest that children and families in child protection cases receive services strongly oriented to support rather than policing activities. The authors note:

> In that context, this study suggests that practitioners believe themselves to be engaged generally in a family support orientation and not in an overly coercive or policing relationship with clients. (p. 140)

Work in the U.K. around family support and accommodation and the related services would support the conclusion from America about the importance of wraparound services. This term is not used in the British literature, but several researchers have drawn attention to the importance of family support services being coordinated by a key social worker who has a relationship with the family, but also puts together a range of other services including practical help and emotional support and therapy. Thoburn et al. (1999) reach the same conclusion in a report on services provided over a 12-month period to a cohort of 200 families referred to social service departments because of concerns about emotional maltreatment and neglect and a comparison group referred for family support services.

From Australia

The Australian evaluations of services described as family preservation services, although not necessarily conforming to the established models (Campbell, 1994; University of Melbourne, 1993, Voight and Tregeagle, 1996), have been small scale and limited in terms of methodological sophistication. A case study approach to evaluation and an attempt to describe different models of family preservation and the linked family reunification are also in evidence (Campbell, 1997a; Jackson, 1996). In this context, Jackson (1996) describes two such models auspiced by the Canterbury Family Centre in Melbourne: (1) a Reconnections Program, in which the child is placed in a residential setting while the family is provided with home-based reunification services and (2) a Family Admissions Program, in which the *family* is placed in a residential setting and receives services with the aim of reunification and/or placement prevention. Descriptive data show that, during the first two years of each program, over half of the families were successfully reunited. At best, these evaluations indicate that family preservation services have a place in the repertoire of interventions that need to be available to child welfare practitioners.

In another study, Campbell (1997b) evaluated a pilot Homebuilders-style program in the state of Victoria. Although the results of the evaluation were inconclusive, the study "did document matters of program development and conceptual interest" (p. 84), such as the issue of the organizational and interorganizational arrangements that can facilitate and sustain service delivery. In addition, the study highlighted issues in adapting such programs to different cultures, including consideration of differences in service systems, in extent and definition of societal and family problems, and in definition of the target population for the service.

Very positively, the evaluation efforts in regard to family preservation services appear to have elevated the issue of service effectiveness and the need for empirical evidence to support new forms of service to a new position on the service agenda in Australia. The expectation now is that new services such as wraparound, the Australian version of Looking after Children, and family group conferences are to be subject to research scrutiny and evaluation from the start. From now on, new services must demonstrate their effectiveness in order to secure continued funding. This outcome appears to stem fairly directly from a decade of effort in the U.S. to evaluate family preservation services. This can only be viewed as a positive indicator for the future, as this harnesses research and evaluation strategies to future service developments.

Family Reunification

From the U.S.

One aspect of out-of-home care services that has been attracting increasing attention is that of family reunification. Maluccio (2000a) and Thomlison, Maluccio and Wright (1996) summarize research on this topic, focusing on recent studies regarding patterns of exit from care, follow-up services and supports, parent-child visiting, recidivism and re-entry of children into care, and the relationship between child's psychosocial functioning and reunification outcomes. The findings reflect the following themes (Thomlison, Maluccio, & Wright, 1996, pp. 129-130):

- Reunification rates from 13% to 90% and re-entry rates from 10% to 33% are reported for children in both short- and long-term out-of-home care.

- Factors affecting exit from care are complex, indicating the importance of targeting interventions on the basis of the different types of exits that children experience.

- Intensive and brief family-centered services positively affect reunification rates.

- Children are more likely to be reunified when parental visits at the level recommended by the courts occur.

- When low levels of both parenting skill and social supports are present, children are most likely to experience reentry into foster care within one year of discharge.

- Children with behavioral or emotional problems are half as likely to be reunited as children without these problems.

As reflected in the above studies and related research (e.g., Walton, 1998), central to the success of family reunification services and the avoidance of further abuse and neglect is the provision of services and supports to the birth family, particularly the parents, before and after a child's discharge from care (Festinger, 1994, 1996). Attempts to address deficits in parenting practices are especially crucial, as confirmed by Festinger's (1996) research with 210 children in New York who exited from foster care, and those who reentered following failed family reunification efforts. This study found that the key predictors of a child's return to care were the parents' limited parenting skills, insufficient knowledge of child development, poor behavior management skills, and lack of support from family, friends, and community.

Given these studies, it seems that parent education and training need to move to a more central position in work with parents and family members of children in out-of -home care, along with more traditional services. U.S. studies of parent education and training have shown that they can be effective with abusive parents as well as with the parents of chronically offending delinquents, especially when implemented with sensitivity into the qualities, needs, and expectations of parents from diverse racial, ethnic, and cultural groups (Wolfe et al., 1981; Banks et al., 1991). Superior results have also been obtained by programs that utilize behavioral approaches rather than simply relying on didactic instructional techniques (Berry, 1988). A later study of the effectiveness of parent education and training programs that compared problem solving versus behavioral training approaches reports that the behavioral training groups produced the best results (Magen & Rose, 1994).

This suggests that participation in a formally constructed parent education and training program may well have to be a fundamental element of a reunification plan. The essential motive is to empower parents and family members so that they can safely reassume responsibility for their children. In describing the Family Empowerment Training (FET) Program, Struhsaker Schatz and Bane (1991) underline these points. They note that the FET program is based on the view that parents of children in out-of-home care must

(1) sustain involvement with and responsibility for their children if at all possible; (2) feel empowered in their role of care takers in order to preserve and possibly reunify their family; (3) become advocates for their children's needs; and 4) believe that they can be good parents for their child while they are in . . . care. (Struhsaker Schatz & Bane, 1991, pp. 671-672)

The added value of a formally constructed program is that it allows parents and family members to meet other parents in a similar position to themselves, that is parents who have lost the custody of their children. Importantly, "when this takes place parents see that they are not alone and that other families have difficulties. Through discussions that arise naturally in these situations, parents experience a sense of community and support" (Ainsworth et al., 1996, p. 41).

As with other aspects of child welfare services, there are also gaps in the research on family reunification, especially in relation to the need to identify effective practice strategies and promote services that lead to positive outcomes. Research needs to address the following questions (Thomlison et al., 1996, p. 133):

- What is necessary in terms of the nature of supports to parents in connection with visiting?

- What services are required for children and families following reunification?

- For what population of children or youth does family reunification work best?

- Are there more or fewer benefits in family reunification for some children at different points in their lives?

- What are the most effective strategies for specific populations (e.g. race, ethnicity, younger- older children, neglected, sexually abused and others) that should be utilized by practitioners?

- What are the critical factors that promote family connections and the effectiveness of reunification? For example, changes in family circumstances, attitude of family members and/or practitioners, types of visitation patterns?

- What intensity and duration of services are needed to produce positive outcomes?

- What role(s) can foster parents play in reunification? Is there a continuing supportive or other role for foster parents after reunification?

To help answer such questions, Fein and Staff (1993) have devised a scheme for conducting a formative or process evaluation of reunification services. The scheme depicts key areas of inquiry such as program efficiency and effectiveness, as well as instruments for identifying potential data sources and obtaining information. As Fein and Staff (1993) also emphasize, *practitioners* as well as researchers need to be involved in the evaluation, thus contributing to the dynamic interaction of research and practice for the purpose of enhancing services to children and families. In this regard, Warsh, Pine, and Maluccio (1996) have developed a self-study guide to strengthening family reunification services that incorporates a substantial evaluation component. The guide is designed to help administrators and practitioners in the efforts to examine their agency's family reunification policies, programs, and services; assess their strengths and limitations; and plan required changes. It is an example of an evaluative tool that can be used directly by agencies in the regular course of providing services, so as to contribute to knowledge building as well as program enhancement.

From the U.K.

There is an overlap between the research on family reunification and the "leaving care" research. Since many young people in care are teenagers, those who are reunified unsuccessfully may return to care, or be users of leaving care services. Although the number of studies is small, they provide fairly comprehensive data on outcomes of family reunification. Thoburn (1994) reviews the evidence on achieving permanence by return to the child's birth family. The main studies are small scale qualitative studies of Thoburn (1980); Trent (1989); and the more extensive later studies of Bullock, Gooch, and Little (1998), Bullock, Little, and Millham (1993), Farmer (1993), Farmer and Parker (1991), and Pinkerton (1994). A range of other studies of care outcomes is also relevant, especially the work of Millham et al. (1986), Packman (1986), and Fisher et al. (1986).

Bullock et al. (1993, 1998) describe a major retrospective study of 875 "returners" to their families from care by combining the cohort of 450 children going into care in the Millham et al. (1986) study with the 321 children studied by Farmer and Parker (1991) and 104 particularly disturbed young people who had been placed in secure treatment centers. This is an important and complex study, which provides detailed descriptive and process data as well as outcome data. Based on the findings, checklists are developed that help practitioners to predict which children and young people are most likely to return home successfully. The authors conclude that around 90% of children looked after by the local authority will either return to their parents or will "age out" and return to their home environment. Sixty-five percent of the returns were rated by the researchers, on a range of outcome measures, as "successful" and 35% "unsuccessful" (including 9% of the total sample who were "oscillators."

Pinkerton's (1994) study describes practice in Northern Ireland and builds on the earlier small-scale studies of Thoburn (1980) and Trent (1989), in order to develop a theoretical model for understanding reunification practice. All emphasize the importance of the notion of "through care"; that is, that good practice starts even before the child leaves home. Reunification in all British studies is associated with contact with the family of origin while the child is in placement.

Farmer and Parker (1991) identify the importance of contracts or agreements as vital ingredients in the model of good practice they advocate. Their proposals are incorporated in the regulations and guidance accompanying the Children Act 1989 in England and Wales. They also conclude that the chances of successful placement back home were increased if social workers maintained a clear sense of purpose, together with a readiness to use authority when appropriate. As with studies of other placements, outcome of placements back with the birth family is closely related to the age at which the child returns home. It also appears that when children return home to a family that includes a younger step- or half-sibling, the placements are more vulnerable. From her small but very detailed study of children referred to a specialist permanent family placement unit who subsequently were placed with parents or relatives, Trent (1989) concluded that when age at placement is controlled for, the proportion of placements breaking down is the same for those returning to the family as for those being placed with substitute families for adoption or permanent foster care. This study is of importance because the quality of the work provided to children reunified was as high as the quality of the services provided to those placed in substitute families. Most studies note that, when children return home, they generally receive a lower level of service than those placed in substitute families.

From Australia

There is an absence of formal Australian studies of family reunification in spite of overwhelming evidence that most children placed in out-of-home care are eventually reunited with their families (Department of Community Services, 1996; Bandt et al., 1996). On the other hand, Fernandez (1996) reports in her study of decision making in 294 child protection case in New South Wales a reunification rate of only 19.1% (56 cases). However, these data are from 1980-1984, an era when reunification policies were less in evidence. Some brief data about reunification rates can be also obtained from the evaluations of Australian family preservation services (Campbell, 1994; University of Melbourne, 1993; Voigt & Tregeagle, 1996), although these evaluations are not designed to identify the factors which contribute to the success, or otherwise, of family reunification.

However, in the Campbell (1994) evaluation of the Families First program, 32 of the 46 children who received service were still at home with their families three months after case closure. A similar proportion of those for whom 12 months had elapsed since case closure by the end of the evaluation period were also still at home.

Stouter claims of effectiveness are made for the Barnardos Temporary Family Care program in New South Wales that is presented as comparable to U.S. family preservation programs (Voigt & Tregeale, 1996). Unfortunately, these claims are not supported with empirical data.

In spite of the prevalence of reunification practice in Australian child welfare, the paucity of written materials about this issue has to be noted. This deficit is further emphasized by the fact that reunification practice is not referenced in Goddard and Carew's (1993) Australian text on child welfare. A more recent article on the policy and practice of family reunification also highlights the absence of Australian materials (Ainsworth & Maluccio, 1998).

Preparation for Independent Living

There is an overlap between studies of family reunification and research on leaving care services or preparation for independent living. The reader is, therefore, urged to look also at the earlier section on family reunification. In addition, a review of selected studies on the perspectives of youths in foster care is provided by Curran and Pecora (2000).

From the U.S.

The proportion of adolescents in family foster care and residential treatment in the U.S. increased rapidly in the 1980s, "as the permanency planning movement initially resulted in keeping younger children out-of-care, reuniting them with their biological families following placements, or placing them in adoption or other permanent plans" (Maluccio et al., 1990, p. 6). Currently, adolescents still constitute a major group in the foster care population, although their proportion is lower due to the marked rise in the number of younger children in foster care. Adolescents represent three different groups: those who were placed at an early age and have remained in the same foster home; those who were placed at an early age and have been moving from one placement to another; and those who were placed first as teenagers, usually because of their behavioral or relationship problems.

Most adolescents in family foster care are discharged to another plan, typically some form of independent living, upon reaching majority age at 18. Unlike the situation in the U.K., in the U.S. few young people in family foster care remain formally with their foster families upon reaching age 18. (The exception involves youths who go on to college or other formal educational program or young people whose foster parents have been granted legal guardianship.) In contrast, in the U.K. child welfare policy encourages young people to remain with their foster families even after they have "aged out" of care or accommodation on reaching the age 18. Foster parents are encouraged to retain a supportive role and the Children Act 1989 allows for financial and practical help to be made available by local authorities to care leavers and their foster parents. These provisions will be further strengthened by the leaving care bill likely to be enacted in 2000. Although it is unrealistic in our society to expect people to be independent at 18, readiness to function independently is another criterion that has been used in studies of the effectiveness of family foster care. As described below, the results have largely been negative, in sharp contrast to the more positive findings of studies cited in an earlier section that compared the functioning of foster care graduates with that of their peers in the general population.[3]

First, foster parents and social workers have consistently reported that most adolescents approaching emancipation are unprepared for independent living (cf. Fein et al., 1990). Second, follow-up studies of young people who grew up in out-of-home placement have also pointed to their lack of preparation for life after foster care. For example, former foster care youths have consistently highlighted their needs in the following areas: interpersonal skills, money management, planning a budget, job training, finding a job, maintaining a household, learning to shop, and maintaining family ties (Barth, 1990; Cook, 1997; Dumaret et al., 1997; McMillen & Tucker, 1999; Mech & Rycraft, 1995). Similarly, in a review of selected studies of the views of foster care alumni, Curran and Pecora (2000) found that two central themes emerged: first, foster children would like adequate information about their family histories and, second, foster care graduates are greatly disturbed by the lack of planning and preparation for leaving care.

Third, and most important, it has been found that a high number of homeless persons have a history of foster care placement, with some having been placed in both foster family and residential settings. For instance, 38% of the homeless in Minneapolis (Piliavin et al., 1987) and 23% of those in New York (Susser et al., 1987) reported a history of foster care placement during their childhood and/or adolescence. Similarly, Roman and Wolfe (1997) found that persons with a history of foster care placement were overrepresented in the homeless population.

The challenges in regard to preparation for independent living include preparing youths earlier in their placement; obtaining flexible funding for work study programs; offering better vocational assessment and training; providing adequate health care; helping youths to develop life skills; and maintaining supports to young people as they move into adulthood (Barth, 1990; Cook, 1997; Maluccio et al., 1990; Mech & Rycraft, 1995; Nollan et al., 2000). Such a panoply of services is required, as adolescents in foster care generally have limited supports in their families and social networks and are often emotionally, intellectually, and physically delayed from a developmental perspective.

In this connection, it should be noted that the concept of *independent living* has been criticized, especially since it creates unrealistic and unfair expectations of adolescents who have left or are preparing to leave foster care (Maluccio et al., 1990; Ainsworth, 1987). It has been proposed that we emphasize, instead, the concept of *interdependent* living in practice with young people in foster care. Such a concept reflects the assumption that human beings are interdependent, "that is, able to relate to—and function with—others, using community influences and resources, and being able to carry out management tasks of daily life and having a productive quality of life through positive interactions with individuals, groups, organizations, and social systems" (Maluccio et al., 1990, p. 10).

From the U.K.

The "Dartington" cohort studies of Bullock and colleagues, which have been described more fully in the previous section on family reunification (Bullock, Little, & Millham, 1993; Bullock, Little & Millham, 1998; and Bullock, Gooch, & Little, 1998), include important data on some young people who move into independent living.

In this section, we concentrate on young people who leave care at the ages of 16 and 17. Studies of children leaving care are well advanced in the U.K. and go back to the small-scale descriptive studies of Godek (1976) and Mulvey (1977). Most prospective studies of children in care (most importantly those of Millham et al., 1986; Rowe et al., 1989, and Triseliotis et al., 1995) include sections on the circumstances of young people leaving care. However, the most important series of studies on services provided specifically for care leavers are those of Stein and his colleagues (Stein & Carey, 1986; Biehal et al., 1995). The first of these drew attention to the practical and skills needs of young people and found that leaving care schemes succeeded fairly well in these respects (Stein & Carey, 1986). However, they were less successful in meeting the needs of the young people for "interdependence." The authors described the loneliness which often led the youngsters to move out of their housing schemes to less suitable shared accommodation and relationships which left them more vulnerable.

The second of these studies (Biehal et al., 1995) is a detailed investigation of four different schemes for young people 16–19 years of age leaving family foster or residential care. The study starts from the viewpoint that leaving care is a process rather than a single discrete event. It uses quantitative outcome measures, but also more subjective measures such as satisfaction. Detailed interviews were conducted with a sample of 42 young people from a cohort of 183 involved in the care leaver schemes. The same interview data were also collected from a comparison group of 32 care leavers not involved in independent living projects. As with most of the British studies, the sample is biased toward those leaving from group care settings, since these are the major users of projects. Those leaving from task-centered foster care also move on to such schemes, but young people who age out of care at 18 from stable long-term foster homes tend to be underrepresented.

For the full cohort in the above study, file data are available, and for the project and comparison groups detailed interviews were undertaken with the young people, the social worker for the child and, for the "intervention" group, the scheme workers. Methodological problems result from sample loss and "contamination," with some of the comparison group joining a project before the date of follow-up two years after the first interviews. Outcome data were collected on accommodation, life skills, educational patterns and achievement, career paths, family links, identity, substance misuse, offending, peer and partner relationships, and pregnancy and births. Those participating in the schemes were less likely to have positive links with family members and were more likely to have left care at a younger age than the comparison group. However, they were in more suitable accommodation and more likely to have improved life skills than their peers who did not join schemes. Educational achievement for both groups was poor, as were their early employment careers. Particularly disturbing was the finding that within 24 months of leaving care, one-third of the young people had become parents (46.5% of the 45 females within the sample in contrast to the 5% rate of becoming a lone mother for 15–19 year old women in the population as a whole).

On the positive side, in common with the researchers whose work is reported in the family reunification section, a high proportion (81%) of all the care leavers had some contact with their families in the early months after leaving care and two-thirds saw family members at least weekly. Only one-third of the young people who had been fostered continued to receive ongoing support from foster carers when they first left care, and within 18-24 months this figure had fallen to less than one-fifth. Thus, foster care placements in this study did not provide a home base for these young people. This is to a large extent explained by the way in which the sample was collected, since those in long-term stable foster care "age out" at 18 and do not need leaving care projects.

Less successful outcomes in areas other than life skills and the quality of accommodation were associated not with the schemes themselves, but with neglectful and abusive childhoods and lack of stable relationships. More successful outcomes were associated with supportive relationships with family members or former carers. One result of these studies has been the "Quality Protects" target for local authorities, to encourage more young people to remain looked after within the care system until the age of 18 and for any necessary schemes to be within the broader remit and resources of the care authorities and voluntary agencies. Biehal et al. (1995) and Marsh (1999) who, from interviews with a more broadly drawn sample of 16– to 18-year-olds leaving care and similar conclusions, pull out lessons for social work practice. Marsh found that although most young people could name someone who was especially important to them, less than half of their social workers knew who this was. Emphasis is placed on the importance of the role of social workers in fostering links between the young people, their relatives, and their former carers, and involving these in the process of reviewing care and leaving care plans.

Also of interest is a qualitative study by Biehal, Clayden, and Byford (2000), which evaluated the work of an adolescent support team in a local authority. The researchers collected data on 56 16- to 17-year-olds referred to the agency for preventive services, through focus groups with staff members, a cost analysis, and intensive interviews with the young people and their families. They concluded that the team was effective in preventing out-of-home placement and recommended the establishment of "multidisciplinary youth teams" in the continuum of services for young people.

From Australia

The only comparable Australian study of leaving care services is that undertaken by Cashmore and Paxman (1996) for the New South Wales Department of Community Services. This is a longitudinal study of approximately 100 wards who were interviewed as they left care and at three months and twelve months post care. The study highlights issues comparable to those identified by Biehal et al. (1995) in their British study.

The young people in New South Wales were ill-prepared for independence. They had experienced multiple placements and lacked stability, which was further compounded by residential mobility after discharge from care. On average, the 47 care leavers, of whom just over half were male, changed their residential address three times within one year of exiting from care. Noticeably, the more times the young people had moved while in care, the more times they moved after leaving care. There were also problems of substance abuse, depression, and physical and mental illness. In addition, these youths had low educational achievements and few job skills, resulting in high levels of unemployment and lack of stable income. After discharge, the majority of these young people also established or reestablished contact with one or both parents.

As with the British study described in the preceding section (Biehal, Clayden, Stein & Wade, 1995), these young people entered into parenthood very quickly after discharge from care. Of the young women in the study, 30% were pregnant or had young babies by the end of the one-year post care period. This is against the 2% of young women of the same age in the general Australian population.

The above studies provide strong support for the development of post-care services for young people leaving care. Barth and Berry (1994), as a result of their follow-up study in California of young people leaving from foster care, made the same recommendation. Of particular concern must be the evidence about premature parent-hood. Given that early partnership or marriages are especially prone to dissolution and divorce, these findings suggest that the issue of cohabitation and pregnancy should be the firm focus of attention for anyone working with young people about to leave care.

Looking after Children

The "Looking after Children" (LAC) materials are included here even though the LAC system consists primarily of a series of administrative tools designed to improve the quality of care and treatment provided to children and families, rather than a type of service. Looking after Children formats are used widely in the U.K. across foster care, residential programs, and other types of services. The Looking after Children initiative has also received considerable attention outside the U.K., and data generated by these tools are being used in some countries as the basis for outcome research. It is largely for this reason that it is referenced here.

From the U.S.

The "Looking after Children" project is known in the U.S., as several American researchers and child welfare administrators have participated in British conferences focusing on these materials. To the best of our knowledge, however, there has not been any project to use these materials or plan to examine their applicability to child welfare in the U.S.

We should note that, in Canada, the Ontario Ministry of Community and Social Services is supporting a three-year evaluation project in a voluntary Children' Aid Society that is conducting trials of the use of the Assessment and Action Records (AAR) from the Looking After Children materials (Flynn & Biro, 1998). In the first report of empirical findings, this project reports on a comparison of developmental outcomes of 43 cared-for children and those of an approximate comparison group taken from the Canadian National Longitudinal Survey of Children and Youth. The two groups were compared on education, identity, family, and social relationships, and emotional and behavioral development. The findings indicate that the cared-for group were seriously disadvantaged in relation to some indicators of educational success. They also had significantly higher scores on five measures of negative behaviors used to assess emotional and behavioral development than the national comparison group. No statistically significant difference was reported in relation to identity and family and social relationships between the two groups.

From the U.K.

Much of the literature about the "Looking after Children" materials describes their development and the consultation process that went into this (Ward, 1995). As yet, no formal evaluations have appeared on the outcomes for children when this system is used as part of a review and monitoring process. However, several researchers have incorporated the Looking after Children schedules and questionnaires in their child welfare research. Brandon et al. (1999), in a study of 105 children suffering or likely to suffer significant harm, used the Looking after Children dimensions and parts of the schedules to consider whether the well-being of children had improved or deteriorated over a 12-month period. Most of these children remained living with their families of origin, although some were accommodated for short periods during the year. They found that more children's well-being improved than deteriorated on all the eight dimensions. More improvement was noted on the dimension of family relationships and emotional and behavioral development. But there was more deterioration in terms of educational achievement and stability. For most, however, there was no change over the year, whether or not the child remained at home or was looked after away from home.

Bailey, Thoburn, and Wakeham (1999) have worked with one local authority to translate the materials into aggregate data so that the authority can review whether its children have made progress or deteriorated over time on these eight dimensions. Data on these 96 children were included in the first year of the study, the largest group being in the 10–15 age group. The highest ratings were on the dimensions of health and ethnic/cultural identity, and the lowest were on dimensions of family relationships, personal identity, emotional and behavioral development, and educational/intellectual attainment.

In a review of the Looking After Children model, Knight and Caveney (1998) criticize the "Assessment and Action Records"—a key component of these materials—for its normative view of parenting and family life, which, it is argued, impose middle class assumptions on child development and fail to focus on structural factors that lead to poor outcomes for children. Emphasizing that the "Looking After Children" materials cannot be expected to solve societal problems affecting children and families, Jackson (1998) offers a rebuttal of the above argument, asserting that Knight and Caveney misunderstand this assessment model and reflect "a classbound view of parenting which would deny looked after children the chance of a better quality of life than their families experience" (p. 45).

From Australia

The Looking after Children materials have been received in Australia with a fair degree of enthusiasm (Clare, 1997). The Australian state-based child welfare system is subject to criticism about the failure to provide safe, secure, and permanent placements for children in out-of-home care and adequate developmental assistance, especially education and life skills training, for these very vulnerable children (Cashmore & Paxman, 1996; Human Rights and Equal Opportunity Commission, 1997b). The trial of the Looking after Children materials is an attempt to see if this fairly demanding system can improve the quality of care that child welfare authorities are able to provide (Clare & Peerless, 1996).

Wise (1999) reports an evaluation of a pilot project undertaken in an area office of the Victorian Department of Human services. The evaluation was very limited both by sample size (n=17) and because it involved a single group, before and after design. The study was largely qualitative and used interviews face to face and by telephone, in addition to focus groups. Psychometric measures also were included: care provider questionnaire, child interview questionnaire, the adapted Rutter Problem behavior questionnaire, a preschool behavior checklist, and the Coopersmith self-esteem inventory. The numbers were so small that they did not permit statistical analysis. The author concludes as follows:

> On balance outcomes for children recorded after implementation of the LAC Assessment and Action records suggest modest improvement. (p. 41)

> Due to the qualitative nature of the evaluation it is acknowledged that no formal claims can be made regarding the influence of implementing the records on children's outcomes. (p. 42)

While there may be doubts about the transferability of the Looking after Children materials from the U.K. to Australia, especially into state services, the really positive part of this development is the linking of the implementation of these materials to research and evaluation initiatives. Fernandez with Barnardos in New South Wales and Barber with the state government in South Australia, who hold joint Australian Research Council grants for this purpose, are providing important leadership (Owen, 1997). Unlike other imported service initiatives that were heavily marketed (Voight & Tregeagle, 1996) but not evaluated until heavy investments had been made, Looking after Children will be subjected to rigorous examination. This more cautious approach is to be applauded, as it may provide important lessons for other agencies and help them avoid errors in implementation and/or investment. This caution is especially important as this British initiative has not as yet been subjected to rigorous research examination. At this point in time, there is no hard evidence that the Looking after Children approach makes any difference to the quality of care provided to children. The results of the Australian research and evaluation initiatives are eagerly awaited in the U.K. and in other countries that are experimenting with this scheme.

Family Group Decision-Making

From the U.S.

The concept of family group decision making—with its emphasis on the use of family group conferences to develop and implement permanency plans for a child—has been adopted widely in the U.S. and Canada, following its introduction by New Zealand professionals at various North American child welfare conferences and workshops in the late 1980s and early 1990s. In New Zealand, national law requires child welfare agencies to refer every substantiated case of child abuse and neglect for family group conferences. The conference, which is led by a court-appointed "care and protection coordinator," involves family members and relatives, friends, professionals, and others who are in one way or another connected to the family. Its purpose is to help the extended family to reach a decision regarding care of the child in question, following extensive deliberations (Burford & Pennell, 1995). As Pennell and Burford (2000, p. 131) indicate:

> Family group conferencing integrates efforts to advance child and adult safety and strengthens family unity while expanding its meaning."

Various articles have described the philosophy and practice of group decision-making. Pennell and Burford (1994), for example, consider its application in federally funded demonstration projects in diverse communities in Canada. These projects draw on aboriginal and feminist practices to adopt the Family Group Conference within the cultural context of each group. The New Zealand model is also increasingly being adopted in private and public child welfare agencies in the U.S., as a means of promoting involvement of the extended family in the care and protection of children at risk of child abuse and neglect and in out-of-home placement. Connolly and McKenzie (1999) delineate the application of family group conference concepts in the U.S., focusing on a model of decision-making, which they call *Effective Participatory Practice*. These authors critically examine the processes involved in conferencing, including the linking of various modes of empowerment, family participation and partnerships, and the multiple pathways to achieving family group decision-making. Hardin (1996) notes that family group conferences in various formats are beginning to be piloted formally in the U.S. Burford and Hudson (in press) describe selected pilot projects in varied settings in the U.S. and Canada, along with their historical origins.

To date, there has not been formal evaluation of this approach in the U.S., although there are frequent references to its value in the professional literature and at professional conferences. However, practitioners have noted its appeal, especially since emphasis on group decision-making and family group conferences is consonant with the concepts of "user" empowerment, as well as participation of children and families in decisions that affect their lives so dramatically. Hardin (1996), among others, has concluded that family group conferences have an important place in U.S. child welfare services, but he also calls for evaluation of their implementation and outcome.

The growing use of family group conferencing and decision-making as a tool with certain families in diverse practice settings builds on child welfare principles and social work values. In particular, it incorporates a basic value—namely, that every child is entitled to live in a family, preferably her or his own birth family, so as to have the maximum opportunity for growth and development. Through more extensive experience as well as ongoing evaluation of its effectiveness, family group decision-making can contribute to the further refinement of such principles and their coherent and systematic application in social work practice in general. In addition, the process of family group decision-making challenges the child welfare, legal, and court systems to become less adversarial in child protection cases.

From the U.K.

Family group conferences are being used in a range of situations in the U.K.. Some local authorities are using them as part of their family support service for children at risk of needing out-of-home care, or becoming heavily involved in criminal activity. Less frequently, they are used as part of their formal child protection procedures, or reviewing procedures for children looked after, to help them ascertain the degree of risk and to make more appropriate protection plans that are acceptable to the parents, child, and extended family. In other authorities, family group conferences are being used primarily with families of minority origin.

Family group conferences have been fairly extensively researched in recent years in the U.K., the main writers being Morris and Tunnard (1996) and Marsh and Crow (1998). These studies essentially focus on process rather than outcome, although some attempt to measure parent and child outcomes has been made. Lupton and Nixon (1999) offer a critical appraisal of the family group conference approach, with emphasis on its potential for empowering families. They describe research studies that demonstrate the potential of the approach for improving child welfare outcomes. Marsh and Crow (1998) provide an overview of the evaluations of four pilot projects involving 80 conferences and 99 children from 69 families. Because of the diversity of situations, outcome data are complex. For example, of the 99 children, 39 were in care at the time of the conference. The proportion of children who remained in care was similar to that found in other studies, but those who left care were more likely to return to relatives and were less likely to move subsequently. Of the 44 living at home about whom there were child protection concerns, the researchers conclude that the low incidence of reabuse suggests that the children were adequately protected by the Family Group Conference plans. Family members were generally positive, and three-quarters said they would choose to have an FGC in similar circumstances.

Lupton and Stevens (1997) and Lupton and Nixon (1999) describe in greater detail 72 FGCs held in one of the authorities included in the Marsh and Crow (1998) overview. The only parent and child outcome measure used was "satisfaction" of family members with the process. The rate of satisfaction declined from 90% immediately after the conference to 56% three months later. These authors offer a critical appraisal of the family group conference approach, with emphasis on its apparent potential for empowering families. They provide summaries of research studies from New Zealand and the U.K. that demonstrate the potential of the approach for improving child welfare outcomes.

From Australia

Family group conferences as a technique for family decision-making have their origin in the 1989 Children and Young Persons Act in New Zealand, where they are used in juvenile justice and child protection services (Maxwell & Morris, 1992; Ban, 1993). In essence, this approach to practice allows extended family members and other professionals to scrutinize openly the position of statutory authorities. This is done within a clearly specified structure in which families are empowered to make decision about the safety and future conduct of their child. The expectation is that decision-making that centrally involves family members will enhance the effectiveness of any agreed-upon professional intervention (Ban & Swain, 1994a).

To date, at least in Australia, the evaluation of pilot family group conference projects have been qualitative. These evaluations report on the positive response of families to their involvement in a family group conference and their greater sense of control over and input into decisions about what happens to their children (Ban & Swain, 1994b). Systematic evidence about the long-term effectiveness of family group conferences in Australia is not yet available. However, in New Zealand a reduction in the use of out-of-home care placements has been attributed to the use of family group conferences (Maxwell & Morris, 1992). Whether or not this trend has been maintained is unknown. Family group conferences sit comfortably with the shift to a family-centered paradigm in child welfare services (VanderVen & Stuck, 1996). In that respect, outcome studies of the effectiveness of family group conferences are urgently needed.

Shared Family Care

From the U.S.

Foster parents can become allies of birth parents and be actively involved in the service plan for each family, as long as their roles are clarified and they are provided with adequate supports and rewards. In many cases, the foster family can play an integral part in the overall treatment program and provide help to the birth parents.

One emerging approach, known as *shared family care*, involves having birth parents with poor parenting skills live together with their children in foster family or group care, so they can observe and practice parenting in a protective and supporting environment (Barth, 1994b; Barth & Price, 1999). The overall purpose is to help the parents work toward being able to provide independent care to their children. In a related program described as "whole family care," the foster family becomes "an extended family" that can "direct parents in crisis to community resources as well as offer emotional supports while the family reestablished itself" (Nelson, 1992, p. 576).

Although shared family care is fairly new in the U.S., it reflects age-old practices in the African American community and is widely used in Western Europe" (Barth & Price, 1999, p. 104). Since it is so new, it has not been adequately evaluated as yet in the U.S. However, in a few years "this model will have achieved enough maturity to be used in comparative tests against other approaches" (Barth & Price, 1999, p. 105).

From the U.K.

For the U.K., the principles of "shared family care" are so strongly embedded in child placement services that it does not make sense to consider "shared family care" separately from short-term foster care and family support. Readers are referred back to those sections, and particularly to the references to Aldgate and Bradley's (1999) research on respite care; Packman's (1986; 1998) work on accommodation; and Cleaver's (2000) study of family contact arrangements for children in foster care. Family rehabilitation or assessment units, often developed from what used to be called "mother and baby homes," have for many years been providing training, support, and assessment for parents and usually young children in group care settings. They are most often used to assess whether it will be possible to help parents with learning difficulties or mental health problems to provide adequate care for an infant. Alternatively, they are mandated by the courts as a "last chance" for parents to demonstrate improved child care in neglect cases. Some "in house" evaluations are available, but numbers are small and the range of differing needs makes it difficult to identify clear findings about outcome. The use of foster care in similar circumstances is increasing, and this has become an important service provided by some of the independent foster care agencies (Sellick, 1999).

From Australia

We have not identified any examples of formal shared care services in Australia.

Wraparound Services

From the U.S.

In recent years in the U.S., there has been growing interest in the use of "wraparound" services and other individualized service programs, especially in connection with the emphasis on outreach, and preventative programs for children and youth at risk of placement out of their home. Dollard, Evans, Lubrecht, and Schaeffer (1994, p. 118) provide the following definitions:

> Wraparound services is used to describe a philosophy of child- and family-driven service provision.

> Individualized services is used to refer to specific services-

and support-provision approaches developed and implemented to provide wraparound services that are based on the unique and fluid strengths of a given child and family.

Flexible funding is used to refer to specific funding mechanisms and access to funding mechanisms developed in support of individualized services provision.

The concept of wraparound services has been adopted, in particular, for young persons in psychiatric and juvenile delinquency settings. In some communities, these services have been incorporated into the services of public schools and as a means of preventing placement in residential treatment (Maynard-Moody, 1994). The two most extensively documented demonstration of these programs are the Alaska Youth Initiative and Project Wraparound. The Alaska Youth Initiative focused on returning institutionalized young people with severe disturbance to their communities (Burchard et al., 1993). Project Wraparound was a three-year demonstration project targeted at children with chronic severe emotional and behavioral disturbance. The aim was to prevent these children from being placed in special classes, special schools, or residential facilities by providing intensive services to the family (Burchard & Clarke, 1989). These services were sponsored by the Division of Mental Health and Developmental Disability.

More recently, a series of reports have appeared that provide the initial results from wraparound pilot projects in New York State (Evans et al., 1996); Maryland (Hyde et al., 1996); Illinois (Eber et al., 1996); and Florida (Clark et al., 1996). The New York study was sponsored by the Office of Mental Health, while the Illinois project was from the Department of Special Education. Both targeted children with serious emotional disturbances and their families. All of the children were either in out-of-home care or vulnerable to such placement. The Florida project was auspiced by the Florida Health and Rehabilitative Services, and the Maryland initiative was based in Baltimore City as part of a statewide initiative to reform services for children and families.

The above projects focused on children referred for out-of-home placements, those already in placement or those returning from out-of-state residential treatment programs. They uniformly report modest gains for children and families receiving wraparound services by comparison to those receiving traditional categorical services. However, there are important limitations to these studies, as they are usually small scale (ranging from 42 to 132 subjects), and do not generally produce statistically significant results. There is also concern about the groups to which the wraparound recipients were compared. It is not always clear that each group was properly matched on a number of important variables such as gender, ethnic/racial origin, family status, or that the comparison with "traditional" services is legitimate.

Thus, the literature on wraparound services and individualized care remains limited and is composed of program and population descriptions, discussion of implementation issues and as yet limited empirical evidence to support claims for greater effectiveness than traditional services (Bates et al., 1997). Indeed, the early Burchard and Clarke (1989) statement that "at this point in time there is no empirical data to demonstrate the effectiveness of individualized care" (p. 55) remains largely true. Other research results that examine the effectiveness of home-based, multisystemic therapy as an alternative to traditional services for at risk youth are equally unconvincing (Henggler et al., 1992). These studies show statistically significant differences in outcomes, but the comparison is with a nonequivalent type of service.

From the U.K.

As explained in the introductory section, the term "wraparound" service is not used in the U.K. Legislation and regulations require child and family social workers in statutory and voluntary agencies to provide to children "in need" and their families a relationship-based casework service, which encompasses practical help, support, therapy, and out-of-home placement in appropriate combinations. Other statutory service providers, including education, housing, and health services, are required to work in partnership with social workers in providing coordinated practical and therapeutic services. This is especially so for those who are looked after by local authorities or whose names are placed on child protection registers because a case conference or court has concluded that a supervision order or a formally supervised child protection plan is necessary. The reader is therefore referred to earlier sections from the U.K. on family support family reunification and task-centered foster care.

It may also be worth mentioning here the growth of child placement services provided by the independent (not-for-profit and private) sector. These "independents" contract with child welfare authorities to provide a full range of services, including casework for parents and children, support for the foster carers (a range of practical services such as respite), educational support, special education, and therapy. Sellick (1999) describes one large "not-for-profit" independent agency in terms of the types of children they serve; the services they provide, and the satisfaction of the foster carers and the social worker who "purchase" the service. In this agency, consumer satisfaction is generally high, especially in respect of sibling groups, young mothers and their babies, and children with very special needs or challenging behavior. However, there is controversy over the high costs and over the tendency of local authorities to use the service as an emergency provision for children not in need of this specialist resource when no in-house service is available. When an in-house vacancy is found, the authorities often move the child back to the less costly resource, thus adding to the placement instability, which is a major problem of the British short- and intermediate-length foster care system.

From Australia

Australian readers may be less familiar with the concept of wraparound, and there is a problem because definition of its processes remain fluid (Rosenblatt, 1996). Therefore, it is worth citing the core principles that shape these services. The principles are that these services will be community-based, family-focused, and culturally competent; have flexibility in funding and delivery; and be driven by the strengths and needs of the family (Hyde et al., 1996). These principles echo those put forward by Stroul and Friedman (1988) in their proposal for a care system for severely emotionally disturbed children and youths and their families.

The good thing about wraparound or individualized service projects is that they are being subjected to fairly firm research and evaluation at the point of development rather than years after their implementation. Currently, in Australia there is some interest in child welfare circles in wraparound as an alternative to traditional services (Clark, 1997). As yet, wraparound services as defined above are only being talked about rather than implemented, and there are no formal Australian research reports on these types of initiatives.

In a recent article about the place of wraparound or individualized models of care in child welfare, Ainsworth (1999) reports the results of an informal survey of the use of individualized care plans by state authorities in Australia. This survey, conducted by Bath (1998), found "one-off care" funding arrangements for 27 children. This means arrangement to fund a service package designed for a specific child that has been negotiated with a particular agency. Such arrangements have been authored by five state authorities and might be considered wraparound programs. However, all of the arrangements appear to have been the product of ad-hoc planning, as hasty trial-and-error responses to a particular crisis. There was no obvious theoretical or conceptual basis for the arrangements.

Just as with family preservation service and the Looking After Children materials, any wraparound service initiatives need to be carefully piloted and subject to research evaluation prior to any large-scale introduction. This cautious approach may help the U.S. avoid errors in implementation and adaptation and another round of service reform driven by the latest imported "fad and fashion" rather than evidence of service effectiveness.

The issue of flexible service dollars in U.S. wraparound services is also worth additional comment. Giving case managers more discretion and an ability to immediately make funds available to families is attractive. However, the Dollard et al. (1994) analysis of these expenditures suggests that these monies are being used to cover expenditures that are already available to families in Australia from the Department of Social Security (DSS) or from discretionary children's expenditure accounts held by state child welfare departments. This reflects the more generous income support schemes available to Australian families by comparison to those in the U.S. One question has to be: is it these benefits that accrue to the U.S.

families using wraparound services that make the difference? If this is so, then the U.S. results are unlikely to be replicated in Australia since Australian families may already have access to these resources.

Notes

1.   See Lindblad-Goldberg, Dore, and Stern (1998) for a comprehensive guide to home-based services in the field of mental health.

2.   We should add that researchers have found that both caseworkers and consumers value intensive family preservation services. For example, in an intensive study involving a purposive sample of 31 families, Walton and Dodini (1999) reported that consumers and caseworkers were satisfied with the outcome of the service, and that a positive therapeutic relationship between the worker and the client family, along with skill training and concrete services, "contributes most to success of the program" (p. 39). There is, however, a need to incorporate consumer satisfaction more extensively in evaluation of family preservation services. In this regard, Kapp and Vela (1999) review a large number of instruments used to measure satisfaction and consider their application in family preservation services.

3.   It should be noted that some of the studies summarized in this section include not only youths in family foster care, but also some who are in group home residential care.

Conclusion

The challenge of conducting rigorous evaluation of modest innovations in the human services—let alone more complex "social experiments" such as family foster care or family preservation—remains a worthy but elusive goal (Maluccio, 1998). In our efforts to achieve such a goal, as noted in Chapter 1, we should acknowledge the difficulties inherent in doing quantitative research and in following the scientific method as developed in the physical sciences. Yet we should continue to pursue this goal—and also strive to complement the rigorous use of *quantitative* methods with the judicious application of *qualitative* approaches, so as to achieve maximum understanding of the impact of child welfare services on children and families. In addition, such research is most effective if it involves a joint effort of practitioners and researchers:

> We believe that the likelihood of successful researcher-practitioner collaboration will be enhanced greatly if researchers and practitioners share their understanding of the various knowledge needs of practice . . . and appreciate some of the basic design requirements for testing . . . knowledge and studying the effectiveness of interventions. (Rosen et al., 1999, p. 13)

Such collaboration could help to improve our efforts to assess the outcomes of child welfare services and also stimulate the development of useful practice principles and guidelines. At the same time, it would contribute to the integration of research and practice and demonstration of the effectiveness of intervention, as underscored by O'Hare (1991) in relation to the mental health field.

Our review of outcome research in the three countries suggests a number of gaps and recommendations for further research, as considered throughout this volume. By way of summary, we should note that the gaps include limited comparative studies of the outcome of such services as adoption, family foster care, and residential care; and limited attention to the dimension of race and ethnicity. Furthermore, much of the research we have cited has involved

children and young people in specialized programs, perhaps resulting in overly positive or overly negative findings in some of the
studies. These programs are usually well-funded and well-staffed,
which should result in more positive outcomes. On the other hand,
they serve populations of young people who are the most troubled
and might be the most difficult to help. Much of the British research
on leaving care, for example, describes outcomes for those who
joined specialist "leaving care" projects, including many whose
difficult behavior has led to the breakdown of foster or adoptive
placements. Those who "age-out" of foster family care at 18 but
continue to live with—or remain emotionally close to—their foster
parents (and often have fewer problems because of this continuing
support) tend to be underrepresented in research investigations.

As for recommendations for further study, we would suggest greater attention to such areas as the role of race and ethnicity
in child welfare services (cf. Courtney et al., 1996); cohort studies of
populations of children using a range of services, especially longitudinal studies; the issue of placement stability and multiple placements, particularly for youths; outcome patterns for the parents of
children who come to the attention of the child welfare system; the
impact on siblings who remain at home when a sibling is placed in
foster care or adoption; the impact of a child's placement on foster
and adoptive parents and their children; and "birth cohort" studies
and community samples comparing outcomes with those for children and young people living in similar circumstances but not
receiving child welfare interventions.

It would also be useful to undertake more extensive cross-
national research involving not only Australia, Britain, and the U.S.,
but also other western and nonwestern countries.[1] Tran and Aroian
(2000) describe a promising, comprehensive, and multistrategy pro-
cedure for developing cross-cultural research instruments. Our
review reflects differences as well as similarities among the three
countries. The differences are evident in such areas as (1) lower rates
of adoption in Australia and Britain than in the U.S. and (2) kinship
care placements; in the U.S. these tend to be formalized with child
welfare authorities, whereas most such placements are outside the

care system in Britain because of more comprehensive income maintenance and other universalist services. On the other hand, similarities are found in such areas as rates of placement breakdown; the evidence that harm resulting from early privation, deprivation, and maltreatment can sometimes be mended through high quality parenting; but also the indication that long-term (albeit episodic) support and therapy are likely to be needed for some placed children and young persons who have suffered significant harm prior to placement.

We have, in these pages, started to map the territory that each of us knows best. There are still many parts of the picture that are blurred or missing altogether. Indeed, research will always be running to catch up, as societies change and new directions in child welfare policy and practice are embarked upon. We are only too aware that we have barely started on the task of comparing outcomes across national divides. It is our hope that others will join us in taking up the task of learning from outcome research across the world, to improve the life chances of vulnerable children and youths wherever they may be. Promoting positive outcomes for young people is an ongoing challenge for all of us (Reynolds et al., 1999).

Notes

1. As an example, Colton and Williams (1997) review international trends in foster care in a range of different countries.

Appendix: Texts on Child Protective Services

Below are brief annotations of selected texts that include consideration of outcome research in the area of child protective services.

From the U.S.[1]

Berry, M. (1997). *The family at risk: Issues and trends in family preservation services*. Columbia,: University of South Carolina Press.

Berry presents a comprehensive examination of the family preservation movement for children at risk of out-of-home placement and examines related evaluative research. Further extending the proposals by Lindsey, Costin et al., and Waldfogel (noted elsewhere in this Appendix), Berry argues that family preservation programs must go beyond attention to child protection and focus on the employment, housing, and health needs of all families. She emphasizes the importance of providing "front-end" services that support the efforts of all families to care for their children.

Costin, L. B., Karger, H. J., and Stoesz, D. (1996). *The politics of child abuse in America*. New York and Oxford, UK: Oxford University Press.

Building on their research studies as well as the findings of other investigators, Costin, Karger, and Stoesz propose a major restructuring of child abuse policies and services. In particular, they advocate establishment in each locality of a "children's authority." The latter would have "a clear and unambiguous mandate to protect children . . . in a geographically circumscribed catchment area," by incorporating a range of investigation, protection, and family support services (Costin, Karger and Stoesz, 1996, p. 173–174).

Dubowitz, H., & DePanfilis, D. (Eds.). (2000). *Handbook for child protection practice*. Thousand Oaks, CA: Sage Publications.

This handbook on how to work with maltreated children and their families includes references to outcome studies that help delineate "best-practice" principles for responding to reports of child abuse and neglect, assessing risk, and planning intervention.

Lindsey, D. (1994). *The welfare of children.* New York and Oxford, UK: Oxford University Press.

Following an extensive description of the evolution of the child welfare system in the United States and Canada since the 19th century and building on his own studies, Lindsey proposes major policy changes for promoting child functioning and development. These include, in particular, the establishment of a "Child's Future Security" account program—an approach patterned after the Social Security system that would provide a savings account for young persons and insure that they have the funds necessary for adult life, regardless of the economic situation into which they were born. Although it may be difficult to implement in the political and socioeconomic context of the United States, Lindsey's proposal enables us to think boldly about the plight of children born and reared in poverty.

Gilbert, N. (Ed.). (1997). *Combatting child abuse: International perspectives and trends.* New York and Oxford: Oxford University Press.

Gilbert and the other contributors present case studies of social policies and professional practices pertaining to designs of child abuse reporting systems in the U.S., Canada, and Western Europe. The volume can "help researchers and decision-makers deepen their understanding of the social policies and institutional arrangements that frame societal responses to problems of child abuse in different countries" (p. 5).

Melton, G. B., & Barry, F. D. (Eds.) (1994). *Protecting children from abuse and neglect: Foundations for a new national strategy.* New York and London: The Guilford Press.

Building on a range of research studies and a critical examination of current service delivery systems, Melton and Barry and their contributors propose a comprehensive, neighborhood-based, child-centered, family-focused child protection system. Included are specific recommendations for the development, implementation, and evaluation of programs and policies that strengthen families and communities and prevent child maltreatment.

Packard Foundation (Ed.). (1998). Protecting children from abuse and neglect. *The Future of Children*, 8(1), 1–142.

The contributors summarize knowledge and experiences in the area of child protective services. Highlights include reviews of studies that indicate the prevalence of child abuse and neglect and document the consequences for children; examination of the uses of kinship care; and discussion of the challenges in evaluation of service delivery.

Waldfogel, J. (1998). *The future of child protection — How to break the cycle of abuse and neglect*. Cambridge, MA and London: Harvard University Press.

Waldfogel has examined successful child protection reforms in Florida, Iowa, Missouri, and The U.Kf. In particular, she has studied the development of the British child welfare system, highlighting useful lessons in the areas of legislative reform, transformation of social work practice, improvement of services for children in need of protection, and establishment of new preventive services for vulnerable children and families. On the basis of her findings, she argues for revamping the current system of service delivery. The centerpiece of her proposal is a *differential response paradigm* for child protection consisting of the following features:

- a *customized response to families*, built on the availability of skilled social workers who are capable of functioning autonomously;

- a *community-based system of child protection*, in which front line workers have access to services that cross agency lines and the boundaries between the public and private sectors; and

- a *larger role for informal and natural helpers*, based on assessment of the family's needs and available resources.

From the United Kingdom

Some of the extensive British literature in the area of child protection has been integrated in various sections of this text, particularly family preservation, family reunification, and wraparound services.

The Department of Health overview of child protection research (Department of Health, 1995a) and the overview of post-Children Act research (Department of Health, 2000) provide summaries of outcome research on child protection services.

Gough (1993) reviews child abuse interventions from across the world and not just in the U.K. Jones and Ramchandani (1999) review recent studies of interventions in cases of child sexual abuse. Most recently, attention has moved from physical and sexual assaults on children to consideration of the impact of physical and emotional neglect and psychological maltreatment. Stevenson (1998) and Iwaniec (1995) review the research and practice literature on this topic. Cleaver, Unell, and Aldgate (1999) review the literature on the impact of parental mental illness, problem alcohol and drug use, and domestic violence on parenting capacity.

Distinctive features of the British child protection system are the prominence given to government practice guidance, and the strong mandate to involve parents and young people in child protection processes, for example by facilitating their attendance and participation in child protection conference (Thoburn, Lewis, & Shemmings, 1995). New versions of working together under the Children Act 1989 and of the guidance on assessment will be published in 2000 after extensive consultation (Department of Health, 2000a, 2000b). These emphasize the importance of locating child protection services within the framework of universalist and specialist services to meet the needs of children and families under stress.

From Australia

Fernandez, E. (1996). *Significant harm: Unravelling child protection decisions and substitute care careers of children.* Aldershot, UK: Avebury, Ashgate Publishing.

This is the only Australian study that can claim to be an outcome study. The study is based on a purposive sample of 294 children between the age of 6 to 16 years, who had entered care between 1980 and 1984 and spent a minimum of two weeks in care. The study used an accelerated failure time analysis to examine age, sex, family composition and income, accommodation, legal status, type of placement, number of placements, and reasons for entry to care as variables that influence the rate of family reunification.

The aim was to build a model that estimated the probability of the event (reunification) with a given discrete time period dependent upon the strength of the relationship between the event and the explanatory variables listed above. The study reports how certain variables, especially time in care (number of days) and change in placement (number of placements), result in a declining rate of reunification.

Scott, D., and O'Neil, D. (1996). *Beyond child care rescue: Developing family-centered practice at St. Luke.* Melbourne, Australia: Allen and Unwin.

This is a qualitative study of how St. Luke's Family Care, a child welfare agency in the state of Victoria, developed a new model of family-centered practice with "hard-to-reach" families where child abuse and neglect had been substantiated. The model builds on the strengths and potentialities of families, enabling them to retain their children and ensure their well-being.

The study details the outcomes for children and families with whom the above model was successfully used. The authors also consider implications for policy and practice in other agencies serving "at risk" children and families.

Thorpe, D. (1994). *Evaluating child protection.* Buckingham, UK: Open University Press.

This Western Australian study is based on 325 cases of substantiated and "at risk" child protection cases reported to the state child protection authority. The study showed that, beyond the investigation that led to the above classification in over 25% of the cases, no further action was taken. This and other findings which highlighted the excessive use of resources for investigative purposes resulted in a reform of the child protection services in that state.

Cases are now handled differently and at point of referral are either classified as child concern reports (CCR) or child maltreatment allegations (CMA). Only CMAs now receive full investigation. CCRs are treated as parenting or family resource issues where workers offer support services. This reform has allowed Western Australia to remain the only Australian state or territory not to have mandatory reporting of suspected cases of child abuse or neglect.

Notes

1. Parts of this section were adapted from Maluccio (2000b).

References

Achenbach, T. M. (1991). *Manual for the child behavior checklist—4–18*. Burlington: University of Vermont, Department of Psychiatry.

Agathen, J. M., O'Donnell, J., & Wells, S. J. (1999). Evaluating the quality of kinship foster care: Evaluation package. Urbana: Children and Family Research Center, School of Social Work, University of Illinois at Urbana-Champaign.

Ainsworth, F. (1987). The rush to independence: A new tyranny? *Australian Social Work, 41*, 1–5.

Ainsworth, F. (1993). Family preservation services; A cautionary note. *Children Australia, 18*, 10–12

Ainsworth, F. (1997). Tracing the connections between family poverty and problem behaviour in early childhood and adolescence. Some research evidence. *Children Australia, 22,* 27– 30.

Ainsworth, F. (1997). Foster care research in the U.S. and Australia: An update. *Children Australia, 22*, 9–16.

Ainsworth F. (1998). The precarious state of residential child care in Australia. *Social Work Education, 17,* 301–308.

Ainsworth, F. (1999). Social injustice for "at risk" youth and their families. *Children Australia, 24*, 14–18.

Ainsworth, F., & Maluccio, A. N. (1998). The policy and practice of family reunification. *Australian Social Work, 51*, 3–7.

Ainsworth, F., Maluccio, A. N., & Small, R. W. (1996). A framework for family centered group care practice: Guiding principles and practice implications. In D. J. Braziel, (Ed.), *Family focused practice in out-of-home care: A handbook and resource directory* (pp. 35–43). Washington, DC: Child Welfare League of America.

Aldgate, J., Colton, M., Ghate, D., & Heath, A. (1992). Educational attainment and stability in long-term foster care. *Children and Society, 6*, 91–103.

Aldgate, J., & Bradley, M. (1999). *Supporting families through short-term fostering*. London: The Stationery Office.

Alwon, F. J., Cunningham, L. A., Phills, J., Reitz, A. L., Small, R. W., & Waldron, V. M. (2000). The Carolinas project: A comprehensive intervention to support family-centered group care practice. *Residential Treatment for Children & Youth, 17,* 47–62.

American Humane Association and collaborators. (1998). *Assessing outcomes in child welfare services: Principles, concepts, and framework of core indicators.* (A publication of The Casey Outcomes and Decision-Making Project). Englewood, CO: American Humane Association.

Ames Reed, J. (1996/97). Fostering children and young people with learning disabilities: The perspectives of birth children and carers. *Adoption and Fostering, 20,* 36–41.

Ames Reed, J. (1993). *We have learned a lot from them: Foster care for young people with learning disabilities.* Barkingside: Barnados/National Children's Bureau.

Andersen, J. (1997). An advocate's perspective. In R. J. Avery (Ed.), *Adoption policy and special needs children* (pp. 1–12). Westport, CT: Auburn House.

Anderson, G. R., Ryan, A. S., & Leashore, B. R. (Eds.). (1997). *The challenge of permanency planning in a multi-cultural society.* New York: The Haworth Press.

Archer, L., Hicks, L., Little, M., & Mount, K. (1998). Caring for children away from home. *Messages from the research.* Chichester, UK: Wiley.

Audit Commission. (1994). *Seen but not heard: Coordinating child health and social services for children in need.* London: Her Majesty's Stationery Office (HMSO).

Australian Institute for Health and Welfare. (1997). Supported accommodations and assistance program. National data collection. *Annual Report 1996–97.* Canberra, Australia: Author.

Bailey, S., Thoburn, J., & Wakeham, H. (1999). *Using the looking after children dimensions to evaluate children's well-being.* Norwich, UK: University of East Anglia.

Ban, P. (1993). Family decision making: The model as practiced in New Zealand and its relevance for Australia. *Australian Social Work, 46,* 21–25.

Ban, P., & Swain, P. (1994a). Family group conferences: Australia's first project within child protection. Part 1. *Children Australia, 19,* 19–21.

Ban, P., & Swain, P. (1994b). Family group conferences. Putting the "family" back into child protection. Part 2. *Children Australia, 19,* 11–14.

Bandt Gatter & Associates (1996). *Report of the review of out-of-home, preventative and alternative care services.* Perth: Western Australian Government, Department of Family and Children's Services.

Banks, L., Hicks Marlowe, J., Reid, J. B., Paterson, G. R., & Weinrott, M. R. (1991). A comparative evaluation of parent training interventions for families of chronic delinquents. *Journal of Abnormal Child Psychology, 19,* 15–33.

Barbell, K., & Wright, L. (Eds.). (1999). Family foster care in the next century [Special issue]. *Child Welfare, 78,* 1–214.

Barth, R. P. (1990). On their own: The experience of youth leaving foster care. *Child and Adolescent Social Work, 7,* 419–446.

Barth, R. P. (1994a). Adoption research: Building blocks for the next decade. *Child Welfare, 73,* 625–638.

Barth, R. P. (1994b). Shared family care: Child protection and family preservation. *Social Work, 39,* 515–524.

Barth, R. P. & Berry, M. (1994). Implications of research on the welfare of children under permanency planning. In R. P. Barth, J. D. Berrick, & N. Gilbert (Eds.). *Child Welfare Research Review* (Vol. 1, pp. 323–368). New York: Columbia University Press.

Barth, R. P. & Price, A. (1999). Shared family care: Providing services to parents and children placed together in out-of-home care. *Child Welfare, 78,* 88–107.

Bass, L. L., Desser D. A., & Powell, T. Y. (2000). Celebrating change: A scheme for family-centered practice in residential settings. *Residential Treatment for Children & Youth, 17,* 123–137.

Bates, B. C., English, D. J., & Kouidou-Giles, S. (1997). Residential treatment and its alternatives: A review of the literature. *Child and Youth Care Forum, 26,* 7–51.

Bath, H. (1997). Recent trends in the out-of-home care of children in Australia. *Children Australia, 22,* 4–8.

Bath, H. (1998, July). *Summary of individualised care survey data* [Workshop handout]. Association of Childrens' Welfare Agencies conference. Sydney.

Bath, H., & Haapala, D. A. (1993). Intensive family preservation services with abused and neglected children: An examination of group differences. *Child Abuse and Neglect, 17,* 213–225.

Bath, H., & Haapala, D. A. (1994). Family preservation services: What does the outcome research really tell us? *Social Service Review, 68,* 386–404.

Beker, J. (1996). Editorial. *Child and Youth Care Forum, 24,* 213–214.

Benedict, M. I., Zuravin, S., & Stallings, R. Y. (1996). Adult functioning of children who live in kin versus nonrelative family foster care. *Child Welfare, 70,* 529–549.

Bergin, A. E., & Garfield, S. L. (Eds.) (1994). *Handbook of psychotherapy and behavior change* (4th ed.). New York: John Wiley & Sons, Inc.

Berrick, J. D., Needell, B., Barth, R. P. & Jonson-Reid, M. (1998). *The tender years: Toward developmentally sensitive child welfare services for very young children.* New York: Oxford University Press.

Berrick, J. D. & Needell, B. (2000). Recent trends in kinship care: Public policy, payments, and outcomes for children. In P. A. Curtis, G. Dale Jr., & J. C. Kendall (Eds.). *The foster care crisis: Translating research into policy and practice* (pp. 152–174). Lincoln, NE: The University of Nebraska Press, in association with the Child Welfare League of America.

Berridge, D., & Brodie, I. (1998). *Children's homes revisited.* London: Jessica Kingsley.

Berridge, D., & Cleaver, H. (1987). *Foster home breakdown.* Oxford, UK: Basil Blackwell.

Berridge, D., (1997). *Foster care: A research review.* London: HMSO.

Berry, M. (1988). A review of parent training programs in child welfare. *Social Services Review, 62,* 303–323.

Berry, M. (1997). *The family at risk: Issues and trends in family preservation.* Columbia: University of South Carolina Press.

Biehal, N., Clayden, J., & Byford, S. (2000). *Home or away? Supporting young people and families.* London: National Children's Bureau and Joseph Rowntree Foundation.

Biehal, N., Clayden, J., Stein, M., & Wade, J. (1995). *Moving on. Young people and leaving care schemes.* London: HMSO.

Blythe, B., Salley, M. P., & Jayaratne, S. (1994). A review of intensive family preservation research. *Social Work Research, 18,* 213–224.

Boss, P. G., Doherty, W. J., LaRossa, R., Schumm, W. R. & Steinmetz, S. K. (Eds.). (1993). *Sourcebook of family theories and methods: A contextual approach.* New York: Plenum Press.

Brandon, M., Thoburn, J., Lewis, A., & Way, A. (1999). *Safeguarding children with the Children Act 1989.* London: HMSO.

Brindle, D. (1998, October 3). Children's homes staff will have to be trained. *The Guardian,* p. 4.

Brodzinsky, D. M. (1993). Long-term outcomes in adoption. *The Future of Children, 3*(1), 153–166.

Brodzinsky, D. M. & Steiger, C. (1991). Prevalence of adoptees among special education populations. *Journal of Learning Disabilities, 24*(8), 84–89.

Brooks, D., & Webster, D. (1999). Child welfare practice in the United States: Policy, practice and innovations in service delivery. *International Journal of Social Welfare, 8,* 297–307.

Bryant, B., & Snodgrass, R. B. (1990). Therapeutic foster care: Past and present, In P. Meadowcraft & B. A. Trout (Eds.), *Troubled youth in treatment homes: A handbook of therapeutic foster care* (pp. 1–20). Washington, DC: Child Welfare League of America.

Bullock, R. (1999). The Children Act 1948: Residential Care. In O. Stevenson (Ed.), *Child welfare in the UK* (pp. 156–174). Oxford, UK: Blackwell Science.

Bullock, R., Little, M., & Millham, S. (1993). *Going home: The return of children separated from their families.* Aldershot, UK: Dartmouth.

Bullock, R., Little, M., & Millham, S. (1998). *Secure treatment outcomes: The care careers of very difficult adolescents.* Aldershot, UK: Ashgate.

Bullock, R., Gooch, D., & Little, M. (1998). *Children going home. The reunification of families.* Aldershot, UK: Ashgate.

Burchard, J. D., & Clarke, R. T. (1989). Individualized approaches to treatment. Project Wraparound. In A. Agarin, R. Frieldman, A. Duchnowski, K. Kutask, S. Silver, & M. Johnson (Eds.), *Second annual conference proceedings from the children's mental health and policy conference: Building a research base,* (pp. 51–57). Tampa, FL: Research and Training Center for Children's Mental Health, Florida Mental Health Institute, University of Southern Florida.

Burchard, J. D., Burchard, S. N., Sewell, R., & VanDenBerg, J. (1993). *One kid at a time: Evaluative case studies and descriptions of the Alaska Youth Initiatives demonstration project.* CASSP Technical Assistance Center. Washington, DC: Georgetown University Press.

Burford, G., & Hudson, J. (Eds.). (in press). *Family group conferences: Perspectives on policy, practice, and research.* New York: Aldine de Gruyter.

Burford, G., & Pennell, J. (1995). Family group decision-making: An innovation in child and family welfare. In B. Galaway, & J. Hudson (Eds.), *Child welfare systems: Canadian research and policy implications*, (pp. 140–153). Toronto: Thompson Educational Publications.

Bush, M. (1995). Transracial adoption: Factors promoting racial identity and self-esteem. ERIC Clearinghouse.

Caesar, G., Parchment, M., & Berridge, D. (1994). *Black perspectives on services for children in need.* Barkingside, UK: Barnardos/National Children's Bureau.

Cairns, B. (1984). The children's family trust: A unique approach to substitute family care. *British Journal of Social Work, 14,* 457–453.

Campbell, L. (1994). The Families First program in Victoria: Cuckoo or contribution. *Children Australia, 19,* 4–10.

Campbell, L. (1997a). Child neglect and intensive-family-preservation practice. *Families in Society: Journal of Contemporary Human Services, 78,* 280–290.

Campbell, L. (1997b). Translating intensive family preservation services: An Australian perspective. *Child Welfare, 77,* 79–93.

Cannan, C. (1992). *Changing families, changing welfare: Family centres and the welfare state.* London: Harvester Wheatsheaf.

Cashmore, J., & Paxman, M. (1996). *Wards leaving care. A longitudinal study.* Sydney: New South Wales Department of Community Studies.

Child Welfare League of America (1995). *Children's legislative agenda: Budget updates and issue brief.* Washington, DC: Author.

Clare, M. (1997). The UK "Looking after Children" project: Fit for "out-of-home care" practice in Australia. *Children Australia, 22,* 29–35.

Clare, M., & Peerless, H. (1996). *An evaluative study of the UK Looking after Children materials for the out-of-home, preventative and alternative care committee.* Perth, Australia: Department of Family and Children's Services.

Clark, H. B., Lee, B., Prange, M. E., & McDonald B. A. (1996). Children lost within the foster care system: Can wraparound service strategies improve placement outcomes? *Journal of Child and Family Studies, 5,* 39–54.

Clark, R. (1997). *A framework for the development of intensive out-of-home care support services.* Geelong: Deakin University, Deakin Human Services.

Cleaver, H. (2000). *Fostering family contact*. London: HMSO.

Cleaver, H., & Freeman, P. (1995). *Parental perspectives in cases of suspected child abuse*. London: HMSO.

Cleaver, H., Unell, I., & Aldgate, J. (1999). *Children's needs: Parenting capacity*. London: HMSO.

Colton, M. (1988). *Dimensions of substitute care*. Aldershot, UK: Avebury.

Colton, M., & Williams, M. (1997). The nature of foster care: International trends. *Adoption & Fostering, 21*, 44–49.

Connolly, M., & McKenzie, M. (1999). *Effective participatory practice: Family group conferencing in child protection*. New York: Aldine de Gruyter.

Cook, R. J. (1997). Are we helping foster care youth prepare for their future? In J. D. Berrick, R. Barth, & N. Gilbert. *Child Welfare Research Review, 2*, (pp. 201–218). New York: Columbia University Press.

Costin, L. B., Karger, H. J., & Stoesz, D. (1996). *The politics of child abuse in America*. New York: Oxford University Press.

Courtney, M. E., & Maluccio, A. N. (2000). The rationalization of foster care in the twenty-first century. In P. A. Curtis, G. Dale, Jr., & J. C. Kendall (Eds.). *The foster care crisis: Translating research into policy and practice* (pp. 225–242). Lincoln, NE: The University of Nebraska Press, in association with the Child Welfare League of America.

Courtney, M. E., Barth, R. P., Berrick, J. D., Brooks, D., Needell, R., & Park, L. (1996). Race and child welfare services: Past research and future directions. *Child Welfare, 75*, 99–137.

Courtney, M. E., & Needell, B. (1997). Outcomes in kinship care: Lessons from California. In J. D. Berrick, R. D. Barth, and N. Gilbert (Eds.). *Child Welfare Research Review, 2*, (pp. 130–149). New York: Columbia University Press.

Curran, M. C., & Pecora, P. J. (2000). Incorporating the perspectives of youth placed in family foster care: Selected research findings and methodological challenges. In P. A. Curtis, G. Dale, Jr., & J. C. Kendall (Eds.), *The foster care crisis: Translating research into policy and practice* (pp. 99–125). Lincoln, NE: The University of Nebraska Press, in association with the Child Welfare League of America.

Curry, J. F. (1991). Outcome research on residential placements: Implications and suggested directions. *American Journal of Orthopsychiatry, 61*, 348–357.

Curtis, P. A. (Ed.). (1994). A research agenda for child welfare [Special issue]. *Child Welfare, 73*, 353–655.

Delfabbro, P.H., Barber, J.B., & Cooper, L. (2000). Placement disruption and dislocation in South Australian substitute care. *Children Australia, 25,* 16–20.

Department of Community Services (New South Wales, Australia). (1996). *Annual Report.* Sydney: Author

Department of Family and Children's Services (Western Australia). (1996). *Annual Report.* Perth, Western Australia: Author.

Department of Health, England. (1989a). *Patterns and outcomes in child placement.* London: HMSO.

Department of Health, England. (1989b). *Principles and practice in regulations and guidance.* London: HMSO.

Department of Health, England. (1991). *The Children Act 1989. Guidance and regulations: Vol. 3. Family placements.* London: HMSO.

Department of Health, England. (1995a). *Child protection: Messages from research.* London: HMSO.

Department of Health, England. (1995b). *The challenge of partnership in child protection.* London: HMSO.

Department of Health, England. (1996). *Focus on teenagers: Research into practice.* London: HMSO.

Department of Health, England. (1997a). *Children looked after by local authorities: Year ending March 31, 1996.* London: Author.

Department of Health, England. (1997b). *People like us: The report of the review of safeguards for children living away from home.* (The Utting report). London: HMSO.

Department of Health, England. (1998). *Caring for children away from home.* London; HMSO.

Department of Health, England. (1999). *Children looked after by local authorities.* London: HMSO.

Department of Health, England (2000). *The implementation of the Children Act 1989: Messages from research.* London: HMSO.

Department of Health, England. Home Office, Department for Education and Employment, The National Assembly for Wales (2000a). *Working together to safeguard children.* London: HMSO.

Department of Health, England. Home Office, Department for Education and Employment, The National Assembly for Wales (2000b). *Framework for the assessment of children in need and their families.* London: HMSO.

Department of Health, England. Home office. Department for Education and Employment (2000c). *Assessing children in need and their families: Practice guidance.* London: HMSO.

Depp, C. H. (1983). Placing siblings together. *Children Today*, 12, 2 14–19.

Dollard, N., Evans, M. E., Lubrecht, J., & Schaeffer, D. (1994). The use of flexible service dollars in rural community based programs for children with serious emotional disturbance and their families. *Journal of Emotional and Behavioral Disorders, 2*, 117–125.

Downs, S. W., Costin, L. B., & McFadden, E. J. (1996). *Child welfare and family services: Policies and practice* (5th ed.). White Plains, NY: Longman Publishers.

Drisko, J. W. (Ed.). (2000). Clinical Practice Evaluation: Conceptual Issues, Empirical Studies, and Practice Implications [Special Issue]. *Smith College Studies in Social Work, 70*(2).

Dubowitz, H., & DePanfilis, D. (2000). *Handbook for child protection practice.* Thousand Oaks, CA: Sage Publications.

Dumaret, A. C., Coppel-Batsh, M., & Couraud, S. (1997). Adult outcomes of children reared for long-term periods in foster families. *Child Abuse and Neglect, 21*, 911–927.

Dyer, E. M., & Evans, S. W. B. (1997). Family induction into foster care. *Children Australia, 22*, 36–41.

Eber, L., Osuch, R., & Redditt, C. A. (1996). School-based applications of the wraparound process: Early results on service provision and student outcomes. *Journal of Child and Family Studies, 5*, 83–99.

Evans, S. W. B., & Tierney, L. J. (1995). Making foster care possible: A study of 307 foster families in Victoria. *Children Australia, 20*, 4–9.

Evans, M. E., Armstrong, M. I., & Kuppinger, A. D. (1996). Family-centered intensive case management: A step toward understanding individualised care. *Journal of Child and Family, 5*, 55–65.

Ewalt, P. L., Freeman, E. M., & Fortune, A. E. (Eds.). (1999). *Multicultural issues in social work: Practice and research.* Washington, DC: NASW Press.

Fanshel, D., Finch, S. J., & Grundy, J. F. (1989). Modes of exit from foster family care and adjustment at time of departure of children with unstable life histories. *Child Welfare, 68*, 391–402.

Fanshel, D., Finch, S. J., & Grundy, J. F. (1990). *Foster care children in life course perspective.* New York: Columbia University Press.

Fanshel, D., & Shinn, E. B. (1978). *Children in foster care: A longitudinal investigation.* New York: Columbia University Press.

Farmer, E. (1993). Going home: What makes reunification work? In P. Marsh, & J. Triseliotis (Eds.). *Prevention and reunification in child care* (pp. 147–166). London: Batsford.

Farmer, E., & Owen, M. (1995). *Child protection practice: Private risks and public remedies.* London: HMSO.

Farmer, E., & Parker, R. (1991). *Trials and tribulations: Returning children from local authority care to their families.* London: HMSO.

Farmer, E., & Pollock, S. (1998). *Sexually abused and abusing children in substitute care.* Chichester, UK: Wiley.

Fein, E., Maluccio, A.N., Hamilton, V.J., & Ward, D.E. (1983). After foster care: Outcomes of permanency planning for children. *Child Welfare, 62,* 485–562.

Fein, E., Maluccio, A.N., & Kluger, M. (1990). *No more partings — An examination of long-term foster care.* Washington, DC: Child Welfare League of America.

Fein, E. (1991). Issues in foster family care: Where do we stand? *American Journal of Orthopsychiatry, 61,* 578–583.

Fein, E. & Maluccio, A.N. (1991). Foster family care: Solution or problem? In W.A. Rhodes & W.K. Brown (Eds.). *Why some children despite the odds* (pp. 55–66). New York: Praeger Publishers.

Fein, E. & Maluccio, A. N. (1992). Permanency planning: Another remedy in jeopardy? *Social Services Review, 66,* 337–348.

Fein, E. & Staff, E. (1993). The interaction of research and practice in family reunification. In B. A. Pine., Warsh R., & Maluccio A. N. (Eds.). *Together again: Family reunification in foster care.* (pp. 199–212). New York: Child Welfare League of America.

Feldman, L. (1991). *Assessing the effectiveness of family preservation services in New Jersey within an ecological context.* Trenton, NJ: New Jersey Division of Youth and Family Services, Bureau of Research, Evaluation and Quality Assurance.

Fernandez, E. (1996). *Significant harm: Unraveling child protection decisions and substitute care careers of children.* Aldershot, UK: Avebury, Ashgate Publishing.

Festinger, T. (1983). *No one ever asked us: A postscript to foster care.* New York: Columbia University Press.

Festinger, T. (1994). *Returning to care: Discharge and reentry into foster care.* Washington, DC: Child Welfare League of America.

Festinger, T. (1996). Going home and returning to foster care. *Children and Youth Services Review, 8,* 383–402.

Fisher, M., Marsh, P., Phillips, D. & Sainsbury, E. (1986). *In and out of care: The experiences of children, parents and social workers.* London: Batsford.

Fisher, T., Gibbs, I., Sinclair, I., & Wilson K. (2000). Sharing the care: The qualities sought of social workers by foster carers. *Child & Family Social Work, 5,* 225–233.

Fletcher, B. (1993). *What's in a name?* London: Who Cares? Trust.

Flynn, R. J., & Biro, C. (1998). Comparing developmental outcomes for children in care with those of other children in Canada. *Children & Society, 12,* 228–233.

Folman, R. (1998). I was "tooken." How children experience removal from their parents preliminary to placement in foster care. *Adoption Quarterly, 2,* 7–35.

Forell, C. (1991, September 18). *A strong case for ending international adoptions.* The Age, p. 4.

Foster Family-based Treatment Association (1995). *Program standards for treatment foster care.* Teaneck, NJ: Author.

Fratter, J., Rowe, J., Sapsford, D., & Thoburn, J. (1991). *Permanent family placement: A decade of experience.* British Agencies for Adoption and Fostering.

Gardner, F. (2000). Design evaluation: Illuminating social work practice for better outcomes. *Social Work, 45,* 176–182.

Gibbons, J. (1990). *Family support and prevention studies in local areas.* London: HMSO.

Gibbons, J. (Ed.) (1992). *The Children Act 1989 and family support: Principles into practice.* London: Department of Health.

Gibbons, J., Gallagher, B., Bell, C., & Gordon, D. (1995). *Development after physical abuse in early childhood.* London: HMSO.

Gilbert, N. (Ed.) (1997). *Combatting child abuse: International perspectives and trends.* New York: Oxford University Press.

Gilligan, R. (2000). Men as foster carers: A neglected resource? *Adoption and Fostering, 24,* 63–69.

Gleeson, J. P. (1996). Kinship care as a child welfare service: The policy debate in an era of welfare reform. *Child Welfare, 75,* 419–449.

Gleeson, J. P., & Hairston, C. F. (Eds.) (1999). *Kinship care: Improving practice through research.* Washington, DC: CWLA Press.

Gleeson, J. P., O'Donnell, J., & Bonecutter, F. J. (1997). Understanding the complexity of practice in kinship care. *Child Welfare, 76,* 801–826.

Goddard, C. (1996). *Child abuse and child protection.* Melbourne: Churchill Livingstone.

Goddard, C., & Carew, R. (1993). *Responding to children: Child welfare practice.* Melbourne: Longman Cheshire.

Goddard, L. L. (1996). Transracial adoption: Unanswered theoretical and conceptual issues. *Journal of Black Psychology, 22,* 273–281.

Godek, S. (1976). *Leaving care.* Barkingside, UK: Barnardos.

Goerge, R. M. (1990). The reunification process in substitute care. *Social Service Review, 64,* 422–457.

Goerge, R. M., Wulczyn, F., & Harden, A. (2000). Foster care dynamics. In P. A. Curtis, G. Daly, Jr., & J. C. Kendall (Eds.), *The foster care crisis: Translating research into policy and practice* (pp. 17–44). Lincoln, NE: The University of Nebraska Press, in association with the Child Welfare League of America.

Goldstein, H. (1996). *The home on Gorham Street and the voices of its children.* Tuscaloosa: University of Alabama Press.

Gore, C.A. (1994). *The long-term network program report* (June 30, 1993). Cincinnati, OH: New Life Youth Services.

Gough, D. (1993). *Child abuse interventions.* London: HMSO.

Grandparents' Federation. (1998). *Residence Order Allowance Survey.* Harlow: The Grandparents' Federation.

Grimshaw, R., & Berridge, D. (1994). *Educating disruptive children.* London: National Children's Bureau.

Gross, H. E., & Sussman, M. B. (Eds.). (1997). *Families and adoption.* New York: Haworth Press.

Grotevant, H. D., & McRoy, R. G. (1998). *Openness in adoption: Exploring family connections.* Thousand Oaks, CA: Sage Publications.

Groze, V. K. (1996). *Successful adoptive families A longitudinal study of special needs adoption.* Westport, CT: Praeger Publishers.

Hague Convention on Intercountry Adoption, Family Law Regulations. (1997). *Statutory rules*. Canberra, Australia: Australian Government Publishing Service.

Halliday, D., & Darmody, J. (1999). *Partners with families in crisis*. Melbourne, Australia: Spectrum Publications.

Hardin, M. (1996). *Family group conferences in child abuse and neglect cases: Learning from the experience of New Zealand*. Washington, DC: ABA Center on Children and the Law.

Haugaard, J. J., Dorman, K., & Schustack, A. (1997). Transracial adoption. *Adoption Quarterly, 1*, 87–93.

Haugaard, J. J., Wojslawowicz, J. C., & Palmer, M. (1999). Outcomes in adolescent and older-child adoption. *Adoption Quarterly, 3*, 61–69.

Hawkins, R. P., & Breiling, J. (Eds.). (1989). *Therapeutic foster care: Critical issues*. Washington, DC: Child Welfare League of America.

Hazel, M., & Fenyo, A. (1993). *Free to be myself: The development of teenage fostering*. London: Human Service Associates.

Hazel, N. (1981). *A bridge to independence: The Kent Family Placement Project*. Oxford, UK: Blackwell.

Hazel, N. (1990). *Fostering teenagers*. London: The National Foster Care Association.

Heflinger, C. A., Simpkins, C. G., & Combs-Orme, T. (2000). Using the CBCL to determine the clinical status of children in state custody. *Children and Youth Services Review, 22*, 55–73.

Hegar, R. L., & Scannapieco, M. (Eds.) (1999). *Kinship foster care: Policy, practice and research*. New York: Oxford University Press.

Henggler, S. W., Melton, G. B., & Smith, L. A. (1992). Family preservation using multisystemic therapy: An effective alternative to incarcerating serious juvenile offenders. *Journal of Consulting and Clinical Psychology, 6*, 953–961.

Her Majesty's Stationery Office. (1989). *The Children Act 1989*. London: Author.

Hill, M., & Aldgate, J. (Eds.). (1996). *Child welfare services: Developments in law, policy, practice and research*. London: Jessica Kingsley Publications.

Hill, M., Lambert, L., & Triseliotis, J. (1989). *Achieving adoption with love and money*. London: National Children's Bureau.

Hill, M., Nutter, R., Giltinan, D., Hudson, J., & Galoway, B. (1993). A comparative survey of specialist fostering in the UK and North America, *Adoption and Fostering, 17,* 17–22.

Hollingsworth, L. D. (1998). Promoting same-race adoption for children of color. *Social Work, 43,* 104–116.

Hoopes, J. L., Alexander, L.B., Silver, P., Ober, G., & Kirby, N. (1997). Formal adoption of the developmentally vulnerable African-American child: Ten-year outcomes. In H. E. Gross, & M. B. Sussman (Eds.). *Families and adoption* (pp. 131–144). New York: Haworth Press.

Howe, D. (1996). *Adopters on adoption: Reflections of parenthood and children.* London: British Agencies for Adoption and Fostering.

Howe, D. (1997). *Patterns of adoption.* Oxford, UK: Blackwell Science.

Howe, D., & Feast, J. (2000). *Adoption, search and reunion.* London: The Children's Society.

Hudson, J., & Galaway, B. (Eds.). (1989). *Specialist foster care: A normalizing experience.* New York: Haworth Press.

Human Rights and Equal Opportunity Commission (1997a). *Bringing them home: National inquiry into the separation of Aboriginal and Torres Strait Islander children from their families.* Sydney: Author.

Human Rights and Equal Opportunity Commission. (1997b). (Report No. 84). *Seen and heard: Priority for children in the legal process.* Sydney: Author.

Humphreys, M. (1995). *Empty cradles.* London: Corgi Books.

Hyde, K. L., Burchard, J. D., & Woodworth, K. (1996). Wrapping services in an urban setting. *Journal of Child and Family Studies, 5,* 67–82.

Iglehart, A. P., & Becerra, R. M. (1995). *Social services and the ethnic community.* Boston: Allyn and Bacon.

Ingersoll, B. D. (1997). Psychiatric disorders among adopted children: A review and commentary. *Adoption Quarterly, 1,* 57–73.

Intercountry adoption families in Western Australia: The well being of 4–16 year old adoptees (1996, Autumn). *Adoption Australia,* 12–14.

Ivaldi, G. (1998). *Children adopted from care.* London: British Agencies for Adoption and Fostering.

Iwaniec, D. (1995). *The emotionally abused and neglected child.* Chichester, UK: Wiley.

Jackson, A. (1996). The reconnections and family admission programs: Two models for family reunification within Melbourne, Australia. *Community Alternatives: International Journal of Family Care, 8,* 53–75.

Jackson, S. (1998). Looking after children: A new approach or just an exercise in form filling? *British Journal of Social Work, 28,* 45–56.

Jackson, S., & Thomas, N. (1999). *On the move again? What works in creating stability for looked after children.* Essex, UK: Barnardos.

Jones, D., & Ramchandani, P. (1999). *Child sexual abuse: Informing practice from research.* London: HMSO.

Juratowich, D., & Smith, N. (1996). Quality foster care: Who decides? *Children Australia, 21,* 9–12.

Kapp, S.A., & Vela, R.H. (1999). Measuring consumer satisfaction in family preservation services: Identifying instruments domains. *Family Preservation Journal, 4,* 20–37.

Kapp, S. A., Schwartz, I., & Epstein, I. (1994). Adult imprisonment of males released from residential childcare: A longitudinal study. *Residential Treatment of Children and Youth, 12,* 19–36.

Kellogg Foundation. (n.d.). *Families for kids of color: A special report on challenges and opportunities.* Battle Creek, MI: W.K. Kellogg Foundation.

Kelly, G., & Gilligan, R. (2000). *Issues in foster care: Policy, practice and research.* London: Jessica Kingsley Publishers.

Kelly, S., & Blythe, B. J. (2000). Family preservation: A potential not yet realized. *Child Welfare, 79,* 29–42.

Kemp, S. P., & Bodonyi, J. M. (2000). Infants who stay in foster care: Child characteristics and permanency outcomes of legally free children first placed as infants. *Child & Family Social Work, 5,* 95–106.

Keogh, L., & Svensson, U. (1999). Why don't they become foster carers? A study of people who inquire about foster care. *Children Australia, 24,* 13–19.

Kluger, M. P., Alexander, G., & Curtis, P. A. (2000). *What works in child welfare.* Washington, DC: CWLA Press.

Knight, T., & Caveney, S. (1998). Assessment and action records: Will they promote good parenting? *British Journal of Social Work, 28,* 29–43.

Kosonen, M. (1997). Maintaining sibling relationships: Neglected dimension in child care. *British Journal of Social Work, 26,* 809–822.

Kraft, A. D., Palombo, J., Woods, P. K., Mitchell, D., & Schmidt, A. W. (1985). Some theoretical considerations on confidential adoption. Part I: The birth mother. Part II: The adoptive parent. *Child and Adolescent Social Work, 2,* 13–21, 69–82.

Lakin, D. S., & Whitfield, L. (1997). Adoption recruitment: Meeting the needs of waiting children, in R. J. Avery (Ed.), *Adoption policy and special needs children* (pp. 107–126). Westport, CT: Auburn House.

Lambert, L., & Streather, J. (1980). *Children in changing families.* London: Macmillan.

Landsverk, J., & Garland, A. F. (2000). Foster care and pathways to mental health services. In P. A. Curtis, G. Dale Jr., & J. C. Kendall (Eds.), *The foster care crisis: Translating research into policy and practice.* (pp. 193–210). Lincoln, NE: The University of Nebraska Press, in association with the Child Welfare League of America.

Lightburn, A., & Pine, B.A. (1996). Supporting and enhancing the adoption of children with developmental disabilities. *Children and Youth Services Review, 18,* 139–162.

Lindblad-Goldberg, M., Dore, M.A., & Stern, L. (1998). *Creating competence from chaos: A comprehensive guide to home-based services.* New York: W.W. Norton.

Lindsey, D. (1994). Family preservation and child protection: Striking a balance. *Child and Youth Services Review, 16,* 279–294.

Lindsey, D. (1994). *The welfare of children.* New York: Oxford University Press.

Link, K. M. (1996). Permanency outcomes in kinship care: A study of children placed in kinship care in Erie County, New York. *Child Welfare, 75,* 509–528.

Little, M., & Kelly, S. (1995). *A life without problems: The achievements of a therapeutic community.* Aldershot, UK: Arena.

Lupton, C., & Nixon, P. (1999). *Empowering practice? A critical appraisal of the Family Group Conference approach.* Bristol, UK: The Policy Press.

Lupton, C., & Stevens, M. (1997). *Family outcomes: Following through on family group conferences.* Portsmouth, UK: University of Portsmouth, Social Services Research and Information Centre.

Magen, R. H., & Rose, S. D. (1994). Parents in groups: Problem solving versus behavioural skills training. *Research in Social Work, 2,* 172–191.

Maluccio, A. N. (1995). *Book review*, Putting Families First: An experiment in family preservation. *Family Preservation Journal, 1*, 115–117.

Maluccio, A. N. (1998). Assessing child welfare outcomes: The American perspective. *Children & Society, 12*, 161–168.

Maluccio, A. N. (2000a). Foster care and family reunification. In P. A. Curtis, G. Dale, Jr., & J. C. Kendall (Eds.). *The foster care crisis: Translating research into policy and practice* (pp. 211–224). Lincoln, NE: The University of Nebraska Press, in association with the Child Welfare League of America.

Maluccio, A. N. (2000b). The future of child and family welfare: Selected readings. *Child Welfare, 79*, 115–122.

Maluccio, A. N., & Anderson, G. R. (Eds.) (2000). Future challenges and opportunities in child welfare [Special issue]. *Child Welfare, 79*, 1–124.

Maluccio, A. N., & Fein, E. (1985). Growing up in foster care. *Children and Youth Services Review, 7*, 123–136.

Maluccio, A. N., Krieger, R., & Pine, B. A. (1990). Adolescents and their preparation for life after foster family care: An overview. In A. N. Maluccio, R. Krieger, & B. A. Pine (Eds.). *Preparing adolescents for life after foster care* (pp. 5–17). Washington, DC: Child Welfare League of America.

Maluccio, A. N., Pine, B. A., & Warsh, R. (1994). Protecting children by preserving their families. *Children and Youth Services Review, 16*, 295–307.

Marsh, P. (1999). *Leaving care in partnership*. London: HMSO.

Marsh, P., & Crow, G. (1998). *Family group conferences in child welfare*. Oxford, UK: Blackwell Science.

Martin, J. A. (2000). *Foster family care: Theory and practice*. Needham Heights, MA: Allyn & Bacon.

Martin, D. L. (1998). *An annotated guide to adoption research*. Washington, DC: Child Welfare League of America Press.

Massinga, R., & Perry, K. (1994). The Casey Family Program: Factors in effective management of a long-term foster care organization. In J. Blacker (Ed.), *When there is no place like home: Options for children living apart from their natural families* (pp. 163–180). Baltimore, MD: Paul H. Brooks Publishing Co.

Maughan, B., & Pickles, A. (1990). Adopted and illegitimate children growing up. In Robins, L. J. and Rutter, M. (Eds.), *Straight and deviant pathways from childhood to adulthood.* (pp. 36–61). Cambridge: Cambridge University Press.

Maunders, D. (1994). Awakening from the dream: The experience of childhood in Protestant orphan homes in Australia, Canada and the United States, *Child and Youth Care Forum, 23,* 393– 412.

Maxwell, G., & Morris, A. (1992). The family group conference: A new paradigm for making decisions about children and young people. *Children Australia, 17,* 11–14.

Maynard-Moody, C. (1994). Wraparound services for at risk youths in rural schools. *Social Work in Education, 16,* 187–192.

McCauley, C. (1996). *Children in long-term foster care: Emotional and social development.* Aldershot, UK: Avebury.

McCotter, D., & Oxnam, H. (1981). *Children in limbo: An investigation of the circumstances and needs of children in long term care in Western Australia.* Perth, Australia: Department of Community Welfare.

McCroskey, J., & Meezan, W. (1997). *Family preservation and family functioning.* Washington, DC: Child Welfare League of America.

McDonald, T. P., Allen, R. J., Westerfelt A., & Piliavin I. (1996). *Assessing the long-term effects of foster care: A research synthesis.* Washington, DC: Child Welfare League of America.

McKenzie, J. K. (1993). Adoption of children with special needs. In *The future of children, 3*(1), 62–76.

McKenzie, R. B. (1997). Orphanage alumni: How they have done and how they evaluate their experience. *Child and Youth Care Forum, 26,* 87–111.

McKenzie, R. B. (1998). *Rethinking orphanages for the 21ˢᵗ century.* Thousand Oaks, CA: Sage Publications.

McMillen, J. C., & Tucker, J. (1999). The status of older adolescents at exit from out-of-home care. *Child Welfare, 78,* 339–360.

McRoy, R. G. (1999). *Special needs adoptions: Practice issues.* New York: Garland Publishing.

McRoy, R. G., Oglesby, Z., & Grape, H. (1997). Achieving same-race adoptive placements for African-American children: Culturally sensitive practice approaches. *Child Welfare, 76,* 85–104.

McWhinnie, A. (1967). *Adopted children: How they grow up. A study of their adjustments as adults.* London/New York: Routledge and Kegan Paul.

Meadowcroft, P., & Trout, B. A. (Eds.) (1990). *Troubled youth in treatment foster homes: A handbook of therapeutic foster care.* Washington, DC: Child Welfare League of America.

Mech, E. V., & Rycraft, J. R. (1995). *Preparing youths for adult living: Proceedings of an invitational research conference.* Washington, DC: Child Welfare League of America.

Meezan, W., & McCroskey, J. (1996). Improving family functioning through family preservation services: Results of the Los Angeles experiment. *Family Preservation Journal, 2,* 1, 9–29.

Melton, G. B., & Barry, F. D. (1994). *Protecting children from abuse and neglect: Foundations for a new national strategy.* New York and London: The Guilford Press.

Melton, G. B., Lyons, P. M., & Spaulding W. J. (1998). *No place to go: The civil commitment of minors.* Lincoln: University of Nebraska Press.

Millham, S., Bullock, R., Hosie, K., & Little, M. (1986). *Lost in care: The problem of maintaining links between children in care and their families.* Aldershot, UK: Gower.

Moore, M. (1999). *Successful placements in specialised home based care.* Unpublished master's thesis, University of Melbourne, Australia.

Morris, J., & Tunnard, J. (Eds.) (1996). *Family group conferences: Messages from UK Practice and Research.* London: Family Rights Group.

Moyle, H., & Gibson, D. (Eds.). (1997). *Australian's welfare 1997: Services and assistance.* Canberra: Australian Institute for Health and Welfare.

Mulvey, T. (1977). *After care, who cares?* Colchester, UK: University of Essex.

Needell, B., & Gilbert, N. (1997). Child welfare and the extended family. In J. D. Berrick, R. D. Barth, & N. Gilbert (Eds.), *Child Welfare Research Review: Volume 2* (pp. 85–99). New York: Columbia University Press.

Needell, B., Webster, D., Barth, R. P., Armijo, M., & Fox, A. (1998). *Performance indicators for child welfare services in California (1997).* Berkeley, CA: University of California, School of Social Welfare, Child Welfare Research Center.

Nelson, E. K. (1996). *Book review,* Putting families first: An experiment in family preservation. *Family Preservation Journal, 1,* 117–118.

Nelson, K. M. (1992). Fostering homeless children and their parents too: The emergence of whole family care. *Child Welfare, 71,* 575–584.

Neil, E. (1999). The sibling relationships of adopted children and patterns of contact after adoption. In A. Mullender (Ed.), *We are family: Sibling relationships in placement and beyond.* (pp. 50–67). London: British Agencies for Adoption and Fostering.

Neil, E. (in press). The reasons why young children are placed for adoption: Implications for future identity issues. *Child and Family Social Work.*

Nollan, K. A., Wolf, M., Ansell, D., Burns, J., Barr, L., Copeland, W., & Paddock, G. (2000). Ready or not: Assessing youths' preparedness for independent living. *Child Welfare, 79:* 159–176.

O'Hare, T. M. (1991). Integrating research and practice: A framework for implementation. *Social Work, 36,* 220–223.

Orlin, M. B. (1999, June). *Maryland's subsidized guardianship demonstration project: The first year.* Paper presented at the National Conference on Research in Child Welfare, Seattle, WA.

Owen, L. (1997). Editorial. *Children Australia, 22,* 2–4.

Packard, D. & L. Foundation (Ed.). (1998). Protecting children from abuse and neglect. *The Future of Children, 8*(1), 1–142.

Packman, J. (1986). *Who needs care?* Oxford, England: Blackwell Science.

Packman, J., & Hall, C. (1998). *From care to accommodation: Support, protection and care in child care services.* London: HMSO.

Parton, N. (1997). *Child protection and family support.* London: Routledge.

Pecora, P. J. (1994). Are intensive family preservation services effective? No. In E. Gambrill, & T. J. Stein (Eds.), *Controversial issues in child welfare* (pp. 290–301). Boston, MA: Allyn and Bacon.

Pecora, P. J., Fraser, M. W., Nelson, K. E., McCroskey, J., & Meezan, W. (1995). *Evaluating family based services.* New York: Aldine de Gruyter.

Pecora, P. J., Kingery, K., Downs, A. C., & Nollan, K. (1997). *Examining the effectiveness of family foster care: A select literature review.* Seattle, WA: The Casey Family Program.

Pecora, P. J., Le Prohn, N. C., Nollan, K., Downs, A. C., Wolf, M., Lamont, E., Horn, M., Paddock, G., Adams, W., & Kingery, K. (1998). *How are the children doing? Assessing your outcomes in family foster care.* Seattle, WA: The Casey Family Program.

Pecora, P. J., Whittaker, J. K., Maluccio, A. N., & Barth, R. P. (2000). *The child welfare challenge: Policy, practice, and research* (Revised ed.). New York: Aldine de Gruyter.

Pecora, P. J., Seelig, W., Zirps, F., & Davis, S. (1996). *Quality improvement and evaluation in child welfare agencies: Managing into the next century.* Washington, DC: CWLA Press.

Pennell, J., & Burford, G. (1994). Widening the circle: Family group decision making. *Journal of Child and Youth Care, 9,* 1–11.

Pennell, J., & Burford, G. (2000). Family group decision making: Protecting children and women. *Child Welfare, 79:* 131–158.

Petr, C. G., & Entriken, C. (1995). Service systems barriers to reunification. *Families in Society. Journal of Contemporary Human Services, 76,* 523–533.

Piliavin, I., Sosin, M., & Westerfelt, H. (1987). Conditions contributing to long-term homelessness: An exploratory study. *IRP Discussion Paper No. 853–887.* Madison: University of Wisconsin, Institute for Research on Poverty.

Pinderhughes, E.E. (1996). Toward understanding family readjustment following older child adoption. *Children and Youth Services Review, 18,* 115–138.

Pinderhughes, E. (1997). Developing diversity competence in child welfare and permanency planning. In G. R. Anderson, A. S. Ryan, & B. R. Leashore (Eds.). (1997). *The challenge of permanency planning in a multicultural society* (pp. 19–38). New York: The Haworth Press.

Pinkerton, J. (1994). *In Care at Home.* Aldershot, UK: Avebury.

Pithouse, A., & Tasiran, A. (2000). Local authority family centre intervention: A statistical exploration of services as family support or family control. *Child & Family Social Work, 5,* 129–141.

Pugh, G., & Schofield, G. (1999). Unlocking the past. *Adoption and Fostering, 23,* 7–18.

Raynor, L. (1980). *The adopted child comes of age.* London: Allen and Unwin.

Reynolds, A. J., Walberg, H. J., & Weissberg, R. P. (Eds.). *Promoting positive outcomes: Issues in children's and families' lives.* Washington, DC: CWLA Press.

Riggs, D. (1999, Spring). Sibling ties are worth preserving. *Adoptalk, 2.*

Robinson, C. (1987). Key issues for social workers placing children for family based respite care. *British Journal of Social Work, 17,* 25–84.

Robinson, G. (1998). *Older child adoption.* New York: Crossroads Publishing Co.

Roman, N. P., & Wolfe, P. B. (1997). The relationship between foster care and homelessness. *Public Welfare, 55,* 4–9.

Rose, M. (1990). *Healing hurt minds: The Peper Harrow Experience.* London: Tavistock/Routledge.

Rosen, A., Proctor, E. K., & Staudt, M. M. (1999). Social work research and the quest for knowledge. *Social Work, 23,* 4–14.

Rosenblatt, A. (1996). Bows and ribbons, tape and twine: Wrapping the wraparound process for children with multi-systemic needs. *Journal of Child and Family Studies, 5,* 101–117.

Rosenthal, J. A. (1993). Outcomes of adoption of children with special needs. *The Future of Children,* 3(1), 77–88.

Rosenthal, J. A., & Groze, V. K. (1994). A longitudinal study of special needs adoptive families. *Child Welfare, 73,* 689–704.

Rossi, P. H. (1991). *Evaluating family preservation programs.* New York: Edna McConnell Clark Foundation.

Rowe, J., Cain, H., Hundleby, M., & Keane, A. (1984). *Long-term foster care.* London: Batsford.

Rowe, J., Hundleby, M., & Keane, A. (1989). *Child care now: A survey of placement patterns.* London: British Agencies for Adoption and Fostering.

Rutter, M., & Giller, H. (1983). *Juvenile delinquency: Trends and perspectives.* Harmondsworth, UK: Penguin.

Rutter, M. and the ERA Study Team. (1998). Developmental catch-up and deficit following adoption after severe early deprivation. *Journal of Child Psychology and Psychiatry, 39,* 465–476.

Rykus, J. S., & Hughes, R. C. (1998). *Field guide to child welfare: Placement and permanence* (Vol. 4). Washington, DC: CWLA Press.

Rzepnicki, T. J. (1994). Are intensive family preservation services effective? No. In E. Gambrill, & T. J. Stein (Eds.), *Controversial issues in child welfare* (pp. 303–307). Boston, MA: Allyn and Bacon.

Schofield, G., Beek, M., Sargent, K., with Thoburn, J. (2000). *Growing up in foster care.* London: British Agencies for Adoption and Fostering.

Schuerman, J. R., Rzepnicki, T. L., & Littell, J. (1994). *Putting families first: An experimental in family preservation.* New York: Aldine de Gruyter.

Scott, D. (1993). Introducing family preservation services in Australia: Issues in transplanting programs from the United States. *Children Australia, 18,* 3–9.

Scott, D., & O'Neil, D. (1996). *Beyond child care rescue: Developing family-centred practice at St. Luke.* Melbourne, Australia: Allen and Unwin.

Sellick, C. (1992). *Supporting short-term carers.* Aldershot, UK: Avebury.

Sellick, C. (1999). Independent fostering agencies: Providing high quality services to children and carers? *Adoption and Fostering, 24,* 7–14.

Sellick, C., & Thoburn, J. (1996). *What works in family placements.* Barkingside, UK: Barnardos.

Sharma, A. R., McGue, M. K., & Benson, P. L. (1996a). The emotional and behavioral adjustment of United States adopted adolescents: Part 1— An overview. *Children and Youth Services Review, 18,* 83–100.

Sharma, A. R., McGue, M. K., & Benson, P. L. (1996b). The emotional and behavioral adjustment of United States adopted adolescents: Part II— Age at adoption. *Children and Youth Services Review, 18,* 101–114.

Shaw, M., & Hipgrave, T. (1983). *Specialist Fostering.* London: Batsford.

Shaw, M., & Hipgrave, T. (1989). Young people and their carers in specialist fostering. *Adoption and Fostering, 13,* 11–17.

Silverman, A. R. (1993). Outcomes of transracial adoption. *The Future of Children, 3*(1), 104–118.

Simms, M. D., Freundlich, M., Battistelli, E. S., & Kaufman, N.D. (1999). Delivering health care and mental health care services for children in family foster care after welfare and health care reform. *Child Welfare, 78,* 166–183.

Simon, R. J., Alstein, H., & Melli, M. S. (1994). *The case for transracial adoption.* Washington, DC: American University Press.

Sinclair, I., & Gibbs, I. (1998). *Children's homes: A study of diversity.* Chichester, UK: Wiley.

Smith, J. (1997). *The realities of adoption.* Lanham, NY: Madison Books.

Smith, M. C. (1996). An exploratory survey of foster mother and caseworker attitudes about sibling placement. *Child Welfare, 75,* 357–375.

Smith, S. A., & Howard, J. A. (1999). *Promoting successful adoptions: Practice with troubled families.* Thousand Oaks, CA: Sage Publications.

Smith, T. (1996). *Family centres.* London: HMSO.

Smokowsky, P. R., & Wodarsky, J. S. (1996). The effectiveness of child welfare services for poor, neglected children: A review of the empirical evidence. *Research on Social Work Practice, 6,* 504–523.

Smyer, M. A., Gatz, M., Simi, N. L., & Pedersen, N. L. (1998). Childhood adoption: Long-term effects in adulthood. *Psychiatry, 61,* 191–205.

Stalker, K. (1990). *Share the care: An evaluation of a family based respite care service*. London: Jessica Kingsley.

Stein, J. (1995). *Residential treatment of adolescents and children*. Chicago: Nelson-Hall Publishers.

Stein, M., & Carey, K. (1986). *Leaving care*. Oxford, UK: Blackwell.

Stevenson, O. (1998). *Neglected children: Issues and dilemmas*. Oxford, UK: Blackwell Science.

Stevenson, O. (Ed.). (1999). *Child welfare in the United Kingdom: 1994–1998*. Oxford, UK: Blackwell Science.

Susser, E., Struening, E. L., & Conover, S. (1987). Childhood experiences of homeless men. *American Journal of Psychiatry, 144*, 1599–1601.

Stroul, B. A., & Friedman, R. M. (1988). Principles for a system of care. *Children Today, 28*, 11–15.

Struhsaker Schatz, M., & Bane, W. (1991). Empowering the parents of children in substitute care: A training model. *Child Welfare, 70*, 665–678.

Testa, M. F. (1992). Conditions of risk for substitute care. *Children and Youth Services Review, 14*, 27–36.

Testa, M. F. (1997). Kinship foster care in Illinois. In J. D. Berrick, R. Barth, & N. Gilbert (Eds.), *Child welfare research review: Volume 2* (pp. 101–129). New York: Columbia University Press.

Testa, M. F. (1999). *Subsidized guardianship: Testing an idea whose time has come*. Paper presented at the National Conference on Research in Child Welfare, Seattle, WA, June 1999.

Testa, M. F. & Rolock, N. (1999). Professional foster care: A future worth pursuing? *Child Welfare, 78*, 108–124.

Thoburn, J. (1980). *Captive clients*. London: Routledge and Kegan Paul.

Thoburn, J. (1990). *Success and failure in permanent family placement*. Aldershot, UK: Gower.

Thoburn, J. (1991). Evaluating placements: Survey findings and conclusions. In J. Fratter, J. Rowe, & J. Thoburn (Eds.), *Permanent family placement: A decade of experience* (pp. 34–57). London: British Agencies or Adoption and Fostering.

Thoburn, J. (1994). *Child placement: Principles and practice*. Aldershot, UK: Ashgate.

Thoburn, J. (1999). Trends in foster care and adoption. In O. Stevenson (Ed.), *Child welfare in the UK* (pp. 121–155). Oxford, UK: Blackwell Science.

Thoburn, J., Lewis, A., & Shemmings, D. (1995). *Paternalism or partnership? Family involvement in the child protection process.* London: HMSO.

Thoburn, J., Norford, L., & Rashid, S. P. (2000). *Permanent family placement for children of minority ethnic origin.* London: Jessica Kingsley Publishers.

Thoburn, J., Wilding, J., & Watson, J. (1999). *Family support in cases of emotional maltreatment and neglect.* London: HMSO.

Thomlison, B. (1995). Treatment foster care and reunification with a family: Children likely to experience family placement and treatment foster care services. In J. Hudson, & B. Galaway (Eds.), *Child welfare in Canada: Research and policy implications* (pp. 194–200). Toronto, ON: Thompson Educational Publishing.

Thomlison, B., Maluccio, A. N., & Wright, L. W. (1996). Protecting children by preserving their families: A selective research perspective on family reunification. *International Journal of Child and Family Welfare, 2,* 127–136.

Thorpe, D. (1994). *Evaluating child protection.* Buckingham, UK and Philadelphia, PA: Open University Press.

Traglia, J. J., Pecora, P. J., Paddock, G., & Wilson, L. (1997). Outcome-oriented case planning in family foster care. *Families in Society: The Journal of Contemporary Human Services, 78,* 453–462.

Tran, T. V., & Aroian, K. J. (2000). Developing cross-cultural research instruments. *Journal of Social Work Research and Evaluation, 1,* 35–48.

Trent, J. (1989). *Homeward bound.* London: Barnardos.

Triseliotis, J., Borland, M., & Hill, M. (2000). *Delivering foster care.* London: British Agencies for Adoption and Fostering.

Triseliotis, J., Borland, M., & Hill, R. (1995). *Teenagers and the social work services.* London: HMSO.

Triseliotis, J., & Russell, J. (1984). *Hard to place: The outcome of adoption and residential care.* London: Heinneman.

Triseliotis, J., Sellick, C., & Short, R. (1995). *Foster care: Theory and practice.* London: Batsford.

Triseliotis, J., Shireman, J., & Hundleby, M. (1997). *Adoption: Theory, policy and practice.* London: Cassell.

Tunnard, J., & Thoburn, J. (1997). *The grandparents' supporters project: An independent evaluation.* Norwich: University of East Anglia/Grandparents' Federation.

Turner, J. (1993). Evaluating family reunification programs. In B. A. Pine, R. Warsh, & A. N. Maluccio (Eds.), _Together again: Family reunification in foster care_ (pp. 179–198). Washington, DC: Child Welfare League of America.

University of Melbourne. (1993). _Families first: Report of the evaluation of the pilot program._ Melbourne, Australia: University of Melbourne, School of Social Work.

U.S. General Accounting Office. (1994). _Residential care: Some high risk youth benefit, but more study needed._ (Available from GAO, P.O. Box 6015, Gaittersburg, MD 20884-6015, U.S.A).

Utting, W. (1991). _Children in the public care._ London: HMSO.

Utting, D. (1995). _Family and parenthood: Supporting families, preventing breakdown._ York, UK: Joseph Rowntree Foundation.

VanderVen, K. & Stuck, E. N. (1996). Preparing agencies and workers for family contract services. _Journal of Child and Youth Care, 10,_ 13–25.

Voigt, L., & Tregeagle, S. (1996). Buy Australian: A local family preservation success. _Children Australia, 21,_ 27–30.

Vollard, J., Baxter, C., & Da Costa, C. (1993). Recruiting out-of-home caregivers for children with an intellectual disability in a shared family care program. _Children Australia, 18,_ 23–27.

Vroegh, K. S. (1997). Transracial adoptees: Developmental status after 17 Years. _American Journal of Orthopsychiatry, 67,_ 568–575.

Wald, M. S. (1988). Family preservation: Are we moving too fast. _Public Welfare, 45,_ 33–46.

Waldfogel, J. (1998). _The future of child protection: How to break the cycle of abuse and neglect._ Cambridge, MA: Harvard University Press.

Walton, E. (1998). In-home, family-focused reunification: A six-year follow-up of a successful experiment. _Social Work Research, 22,_ 205–214.

Walton, E., & Denby, R. W. (1997). Targeting families to receive intensive family preservation services: Assessing the use of imminent risk of placement as a service criterion. _Family Preservation Journal, 2,_ 53–70.

Walton, E., & Dodini, A. C. (1999). Intensive in-home family-based services: Reactions from consumers and providers. _Family Preservation Journal, 4,_ 39–51.

Ward, H. (Ed.). (1995). _Looking after children: Research into practice._ London: HMSO.

Ward, M. (1987). Choosing adoptive families for large sibling groups. *Child Welfare, 66,* 259–268.

Warsh, R., Pine, B. A., & Maluccio, A. N. (1996). *Reconnecting families: A guide to strengthening family reunification services.* Washington, DC: Child Welfare League of America.

Waterhouse, S. (1996). *The organising of foster care services.* London: National Foster Care Association.

Weiner, A., & Weiner, E. (1990). *Expanding the options in child placement: Israel's dependent children in care from infancy to adulthood.* New York: University Press of America.

Wells, K., & Biegel, D. E. (1991). *Family preservation services: Research and evaluation.* Newbury Park, CA: Sage Publications.

Whittaker, J. K. (2000a). The future of residential group care. *Child Welfare, 79,* 59–74.

Whittaker, J. K. (2000b). Reinventing residential child care: An agenda for research and practice. *Residential Treatment for Children & Youth, 17,* 13–30.

Whittaker, J.K., Tripodi, T., & Grasso, A. J. (1990). Youth and family characteristics: Treatment histories, and service outcomes: Some preliminary findings from the Boysville research program. *Child and Youth Services Review, 16,* 139–153.

Whittaker J. K., & Pfeiffer S. J. (1994). Research priorities for residential group care. *Child Welfare, 73,* 583–601.

Wilson, S. (1997). *A study of the experience of young people in care.* Unpublished master's thesis. Brisbane, Australia: University of Queensland.

Wise, S. (1999). *The UK Looking After Children approach in Australia.* Melbourne: Australian Institute of Family Studies.

Wolfe, D. A., Sandler, J., & Kaufman, K. (1981). A competency based training program for child abusers. *Journal of Counseling and Clinical Psychology, 49,* 633–640.

Wulczyn, F. H., & Goerge, R. M. (1992). Foster care in New York and Illinois: The challenge and rapid change. *Social Service Review, 66,* 278–294.

Young, J., Corcoran-Rumppe, K., & Groze, V. (1992). Integrating special needs adoption with residential treatment. *Child Welfare, 71,* 527–535.

Zabar, P., & Angus, G. (1994). *Child abuse and neglect: Reporting and investigating procedures in Australia 1994.* Canberra: Australian Institute of Health and Welfare.

Zmora, N. (1994). *Orphanages reconsidered: Child care institutions in progressive era.* Philadelphia: Temple University Press.

About the Authors

Frank Ainsworth, PhD, is research scholar and lecturer at Edith Cowan University, Perth, Western Australia. His teaching includes research and program evaluation methods. He is well known internationally for his writings about child welfare issues, especially residential care and treatment. His latest book is *Family Centered Group Care: Model Building.* His current research projects are about family conferences in hospital settings and the reason for foster carers ceasing to perform the foster parenting role.

Anthony N. Maluccio, DSW, is professor of social work at Boston College, Chestnut Hill, Massachusetts. His teaching and research interests focus on service delivery and outcome evaluation in the area of child and family, particularly on family preservation, family foster care, and family reunification of children in out-of-home care. He has coauthored a number of books on the above topics, including most recently, *Teaching Family Reunification; Reconnecting Families: A Guide to Strengthening Family Reunification Services;* and *The Child Welfare Challenge: Policy, Practice, and Research.*

June Thoburn, LittD, MSW, is professor of social work and director of the Center for Research on the Child and Family at the University of East Anglia, Norwich, England. She is a qualified social worker and has practiced in the fields of child placement and family social work in England and Canada. Since 1980 she has taught and researched on social policy and all aspects of child and family social work in international context. She has authored *Child Placement: Principles and Practice* and coauthored *Safeguarding Children with the Children Act 1989* and *Permanent Family Placement for Children of Minority Ethnic Origin.*

/